# RICHARD III

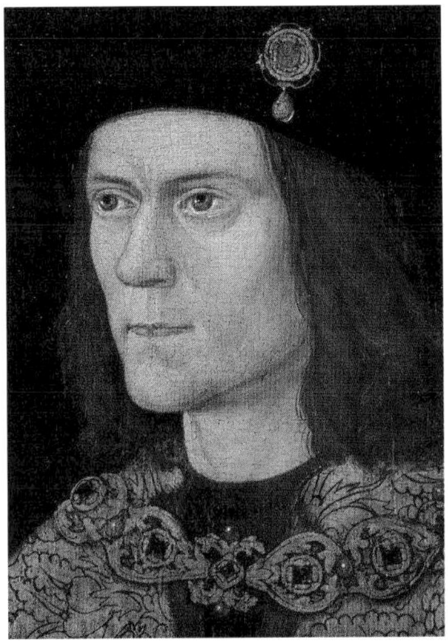

Seynt Edward
England
Francia
Ireland
Gascoyne & Gyan
Walys
The moost myghty prynce Rychard by the grace of god kynge
of yngland and of fraunce and lord of yreland by verey matri
mony without dyscontynewans or any defylynge yn the lawe

**ENGLISH MONARCHS** TREASURES FROM THE NATIONAL ARCHIVES

# RICHARD III

## *A royal enigma*

SEAN CUNNINGHAM

THE NATIONAL ARCHIVES

First published in 2003 by

The National Archives, Kew, Richmond, Surrey TW9 4DU, UK

www.nationalarchives.gov.uk

The National Archives was formed when the Public Record Office and
Historical Manuscripts Commission combined in April 2003



A catalogue record for this book is available from the British Library

ISBN 1 903365 45 7

Designed by Penny Jones and Michael Morris, Brentford, Middlesex

Printed in the UK by Butler and Tanner Ltd, Frome, Somerset

ILLUSTRATIONS

Cover: Portrait of Richard III (detail), artist unknown; Court of King's Bench: *Coram Rege* Roll, 1483 (see p. 103); (background) Richard's letter requesting the Great Seal (see document 9).

Half-title page and page x (facing Preface): Portrait of Richard III, formerly owned by the Paston family. This painting suggests no deformity and may have been copied before 1520 from a contemporary likeness of the King.

Frontispiece: Detail from the *Rous Roll*, portraying Richard III (see document 18).

Title page: Richard III's Great Seal. This impression of the reverse shows the King on horseback. The Seal appears on a grant for seven years to William Hussey, chief justice of the King's Bench, of the manor of Little Barningham, Norfolk, 1485.

Contents page: Court of King's Bench: *Coram Rege* Roll, initial detail (see p. 103). This image of Richard's boar emblem and the Yorkist badge of the 'rose en soleil' appears at the head of the first roll of pleadings (Trinity Term) in Richard's first year as King. These were family and personal badges of the King, and emphasized his dynastic connections to the Yorkist royal family.

# Contents

# Acknowledgements

I would like to thank the many people who have helped in the production of this book, some very directly, others with their expertise, interest and encouragement:

Adrian Ailes, Rowena Archer, Jim Bolton, Paul Brand, Margaret Condon, Jane Crompton, Kate Cunningham, Sandy Grant, Ralph Griffiths, David Grummitt, Steven Gunn, Rosemary Horrox, Hilary Jones, Michael K Jones, Anne Kilminster, Hannes Kleineke, Malcolm Mercer, Stephen O'Connor, Tony Pollard, Deborah Pownall, Colin Richmond, Kathryn Sleight, Anne Sutton, James Travers, Geoffrey Wheeler, and Christopher Whittick.

This book is dedicated to Sandy, who first introduced me to Richard III in 1986, and to my parents John and April for making everything possible.

# Series Note

Most of the key historic documents selected for this series are from the collections at The National Archives; a few are reproduced courtesy of other important national or private repositories.

Each key document is reproduced on a numbered double-page spread with an explanatory introduction placing it in context. (Selected pages or details have been chosen for lengthy items.) Transcripts, with modernized spellings and explanations of archaic words, are provided where necessary. All the documents featured on these spreads are cross-referenced in the main text.

If you would like to see the original documents at The National Archives at Kew, please see www.nationalarchives.gov.uk or phone 020 8392 5200 for information about how to obtain a free Reader's Ticket.

For further information about titles in the ENGLISH MONARCHS series or other publications from The National Archives, please send your name and address to:

Publications Marketing, FREEPOST SEA 7565, Richmond, Surrey, UK TW9 4DU (stamp required from overseas)

To order any publication from The National Archives, visit www.pro.gov.uk/bookshop/

# The Documents

Richards Rex tertius
3

# Preface

Almost everyone has heard of Richard III, and most of us would offer an opinion as to whether he was a virtuous king maligned by history or an evil schemer who murdered his way to the throne. Whatever side of the debate we subscribe to, Richard III is undoubtedly a king fully in the spotlight – surely more has been written about him than any other English monarch, despite his reign of only twenty-six months. The persistent controversy surrounding Richard's personality and motives, life and reign, means unanswerable questions about him will continue to be posed until some new nugget of crucial evidence is uncovered. The Richard III Society continues to try to rehabilitate the King, and its scrutiny of the international media reveals the frequency with which the name, person and image of Richard III is used as a convenient comparison for modern evil, intrigue, plotting and scandal.

The sources for Richard's short life and reign are well known and the facts have been squeezed from them by generations of historians. However, this is where Richard moves out of his place within the fifteenth century and enters a stylized modern re-working of late medieval England, where he has little connection to his period, family, environment or society. We accept Richard either as a manipulated victim of Tudor propaganda, or as the scheming monster of Shakespeare's play, but by promoting these stereotypes, writers and historians have moved inexorably away from whoever the real Richard III actually was, and these distorting ideas have survived through the generations. As an educated and highly literate member of the ruling elite, Richard III helped to promote the ideas, expectations and assumptions that informed the behaviour of fifteenth-century society at all levels. They influenced him just as much as those around him, and to separate Richard from such ideas is to cut him out of his proper environment. This book does not offer any shortcut to the real Richard III, but it does try to set him in his contemporary context, using a selection of the key sources in their original form. This approach may be the solution to avoiding the pitfalls of taking sides in this age-old debate.

# Richard and the Wars of the Roses

## CHILDHOOD AND YOUTH, 1452–65

Ralph Neville, Earl of Westmorland and his surviving children. This image of the Neville family at prayer is from an English *Book of Hours* made for the Nevilles in the second half of the fifteenth century. This powerful noble family dominated the north of England during the period of Yorkist kingship.

Richard Plantagenet was born at Fotheringhay in Northamptonshire on 2 October 1452. He was the youngest son of Cecily Neville, daughter of Ralph, Earl of Westmorland, and Richard, Duke of York, at that time heir presumptive to the throne. As the youngest surviving of twelve children, Richard played no direct part in the turbulent events of the first phase of the Wars of the Roses, but by the time he was eight years old, Richard had experienced at first hand the chaos and danger of civil war.

Richard may only have had a vague impression of the fluctuating fortunes of his father, Richard, Duke of York, as he pressed his claim to the Crown at the end of the 1450s. However, the disruption of the years 1459–61, when Richard was seven and eight years old, must surely have left a strong impression of family unity and self-belief. He may have been present with his mother and brothers when his father was nearly captured at his castle of Ludlow in 1459, and he seems then to have been in his mother's care at Fotheringhay while York remained exiled in Ireland until September 1460.

Richard's eldest brother Edward, Earl of March (later Edward IV), and the Neville earls of Salisbury and Warwick fled to Calais, from where they invaded England and succeeded in capturing Henry VI at the Battle of Northampton in July 1460. Even though the

Ludlow Castle. After the Battle of Blore Heath on 23 September 1459, the victorious Yorkist army of the Earl of Salisbury joined the forces of Warwick and York near York's castle of Ludlow. Two large Lancastrian armies were still nearby, and the rivals again met at Ludford Bridge on 12 October. The best soldiers in York's army were members of the Calais garrison, then under Warwick's control. But with the promise of a pardon from Henry VI they changed sides; the Yorkist captains retreated, and the leaderless Yorkist army dispersed. York fled to Ireland, while the Neville earls of Salisbury and Warwick with Edward, Earl of March, moved to Calais.

Yorkist family had been dispersed, the common belief in York's claim to the Crown was something that probably sustained the family and its supporters through exile, and attainder at the Coventry parliament of November 1459.

When the Duke of York returned from Ireland, he was able to secure an agreement from Parliament that he should be Henry VI's heir, to the exclusion of Edward, Prince of Wales. This caused a resumption of full-scale war, with Queen Margaret raising a massive northern army that outmanoeuvred the Duke of York at Sandal Castle in December 1460. Both York and Richard's brother Edmund, Earl of Rutland died at the subsequent Battle of Wakefield. With Edward, Earl of March now Yorkist claimant to the throne, York's widow Cecily sent Richard and his brother George to safety in the Burgundian Netherlands while the final conflicts of this first stage of the civil wars were played out at the battles of Mortimer's Cross, St Albans and Towton in February and March 1461.

Historical documents can tell us very little of Richard's childhood. He probably spent time with his mother at Fotheringhay and at her London residence, Baynards Castle. There may also have been lodgings for Richard and his brother George (who soon became Duke of Clarence) at royal palaces such as Greenwich, and it is likely that the household of Edward IV bore some of the costs of their upkeep. The first real evidence of Richard's progress and the future role expected of him was the granting of a suitable title in October 1461, when he became Duke of Gloucester. He was also elected to the Order of the Garter in February 1462. Soon after, probably in his twelfth year, he made the deeply significant move to the household of Richard Neville, Earl of Warwick.

Edward, Earl of March and the Neville earls landing in exile at Calais in October 1459 (from a sixteenth-century manuscript). By late June 1460 they were confident of enough support within England to re-invade. On 2 July they entered London and began military preparations for the campaign that ended with the Yorkist victory at Northampton on 10 July.

Henry VI's capture after the Battle of Northampton, 10 July 1460, from an original genealogical roll of Edward IV's reign. Custody of the King in Yorkist hands enabled the Duke of York to press his claim to be heir apparent at the parliament that met in October 1460.

## THE WARD OF WARWICK, 1465–9

By 1465 the junior branch of the Neville family were unchallenged masters of northern England. The accumulation of inherited estates and titles, and the eclipse of the rival Percy family after Towton, meant that there was no more powerful person than Richard Neville, the 'Kingmaker' Earl of Warwick, to complete the education of the King's brother.

Warwick's support for the Yorkist claim had proved decisive in Edward IV's victory, and the King chose him to be Richard's tutor to cement the dynastic strength of the new regime (see document 1, *The Kingmaker's expenses*). Richard familiarized himself with the leaders of northern society as he accompanied Warwick to his northern fortresses of Middleham, Sheriff Hutton, Penrith and Barnard Castle. Although no formal record of his upbringing has survived, Warwick's experience of war, estate management, and high politics must have given Richard an elite, if conventional, schooling.

Sheriff Hutton was one of the major fortresses in the north. It had been redesigned by Sir John Neville after 1382, and was an essential link in the chain of castles that protected Neville dominance of the region. Richard spent some time here as Warwick's ward, and once he assumed Warwick's position in the north after 1471, Sheriff Hutton remained an important stronghold.

# 1 *The Kingmaker's expenses*

This is a Teller's Roll (in Latin) from 1465, recording a payment of £1000 made to the Earl of Warwick for raising Richard of Gloucester and Francis, Lord Lovell, at Middleham. Tellers were officials who counted receipts and issues of cash in the Exchequer. The records featured here were brief summaries of income and expenditure.

Richard Neville, 'The Kingmaker' Earl of Warwick, was Richard of Gloucester's tutor and mentor. He was also a key figure in the establishment of Edward IV on the throne in 1461. Richard's appearance in Warwick's household, with this substantial payment, in the autumn of 1465 when he was about thirteen years old, was a token of the esteem in which Edward IV and the Yorkist royal family held Warwick. It also emphasizes that an education suitable for the young Duke would be found in the household of Warwick and his countess Anne Beauchamp.

The education of a royal prince in the household of a leading courtier was a long established tradition. The Crown bore the costs of the royal education, but it was hoped that the worldly experience and practical qualities of a leading noble would enhance the regal bearing that had already developed during a prince's early childhood.

This period was essential in forming Richard III's character, but we have very little information about how he spent his time. He must have met his future wife Anne, then only nine years old; and he travelled with his guardian, appearing at Warwick and when the Earl's brother George was made Archbishop of York in 1465. It has even been suggested that Richard's alleged deformities were caused by over-enthusiastic practice at archery and swordsmanship while with Warwick. Documents provide no evidence of this. However, the lifelong friendship formed with Francis, Lord Lovell, proved a solid basis for Richard's career as the King's brother.

Richard must also have developed other associations and have gained experience of conducting himself as a major public figure. In particular, the decline of the friendship between Warwick and Edward during the late 1460s must have taught Richard several lessons in how powerful figures conducted themselves: how their acquisitiveness could be manipulated, and how the quality of lordship they exercised determined the durability of friendships in times of crisis.

## THE ROLL READS:

To Richard Earl of Warwick, for costs and expenses incurred by him for the Lord Duke of Gloucester, the King's brother, and for an exhibition [maintenance] &c, of the wardship and marriage [Warwick was entitled to arrange Lovell's marriage] of the son and heir of the Lord de Lovell, £1000.

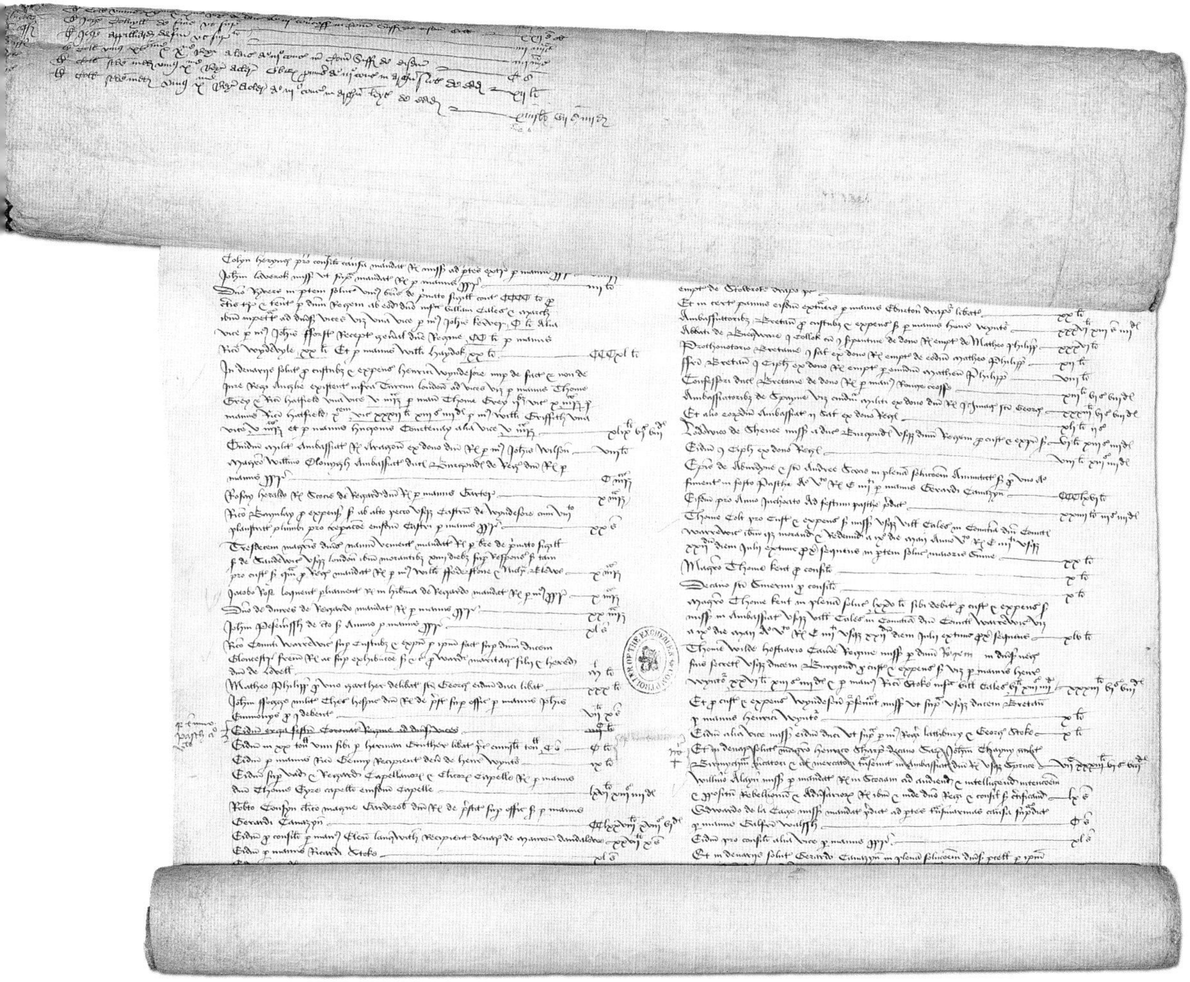

Jean de Wavrin presenting a copy of his *Anciennes Chroniques d'Angleterre* to Edward IV at court. It has been suggested that Richard is the figure in the green hat in the foreground, and that this illustration may be an attempt at a likeness of him in the late 1470s.

Richard stayed in Warwick's company despite a souring of the relationship between the Earl and the King after Edward's marriage to Elizabeth Woodville in 1464. Edward's patronage of the new Queen's family and disagreements over the course of foreign policy served only to drive Warwick further into isolation during the following years.

Richard remained with Warwick until Edward IV brought him back to court early in 1469, just after his sixteenth birthday.

Edward's recall of Richard clearly marked his coming of age in the sense of political responsibility, since he was active on commissions that same year. The King was possibly also aware that Warwick's simmering discontent was likely to influence the teenage Duke if he remained within the Neville household. Within a few months of Richard's return to his brother's side, Warwick led his northern servants in open rebellion, and, ironically, it was the well rewarded Duke of Clarence and not Richard who backed him.

The contacts Richard had developed as Warwick's ward in the north made him an ideal source of knowledge in the King's efforts to defeat him. As a result, Richard was suddenly a vital figure in the royalist party as civil war was renewed in June 1469. By this date, Richard had astutely mastered many of the skills required of a high-ranking patron (read a letter written by Richard at this time; document 2, ***Good lordship***).

## RICHARD COMES OF AGE: REBELLION AND RESPONSIBILITY, 1469–71

Despite spending the formative years of his minority with Warwick, Richard chose to remain loyal to the Yorkist dynasty, rather than follow such private allegiance as he may have retained towards his former tutor. Although his inexperience of high politics may have curbed any deeper involvement, Richard displayed here a strong obligation to his father's vision of a legitimate Yorkist monarchy. This legacy may have been a constant motivation for much of Richard's subsequent political action.

Warwick's Yorkshire followers defeated the King's leading Welsh supporters, the Herberts, at Edgecote on 26 July 1469. Edward IV was captured a few days later, but Warwick was not able to dominate the King as Richard, Duke of York had controlled Henry VI in 1460. Therefore Edward was released from Middleham in early September 1469, possibly after Richard's intervention.

# 2 *Good lordship*

This is the earliest surviving letter written by Richard, Duke of Gloucester. It dates from June 1469 and was written at Castle Rising in Norfolk when Richard was on pilgrimage to Walsingham with Edward IV. The main body of the letter was copied out by a Chancery clerk, but the postscript is in Richard's handwriting.

Richard was sixteen years old at this time and this letter suggests that he had already mastered the techniques of late medieval noble lordship. Richard needs to finance his position in the north of England, and asks for a substantial loan from an unnamed person (possibly Sir John Say of Broxbourne), who had already petitioned the Duke in a separate matter. Richard's personal postscript makes it clear that an advance of the money would secure a favourable response from the Duke in the matter under discussion.

This is an example of one of the basic facts of noble life in the late fifteenth century: that authority depended on the projection of good lordship and the ability of lords to defend servants' interests, but also their confidence that those same servants would support their master when required. That support could take the form of loans, the performance of specific offices or duties, but also in a more general expectation that servants would help to uphold the lord's interests, rights and demands. Richard cultivated all of these key skills of late medieval rulers and built up a powerful network of personal loyalty in lands that he received from the Crown. This experience was essential in forming ties of real personal loyalty and obligation, as demonstrated by the Duke's letters patent giving fees for life service listed in document 3, ***Ties of service***.

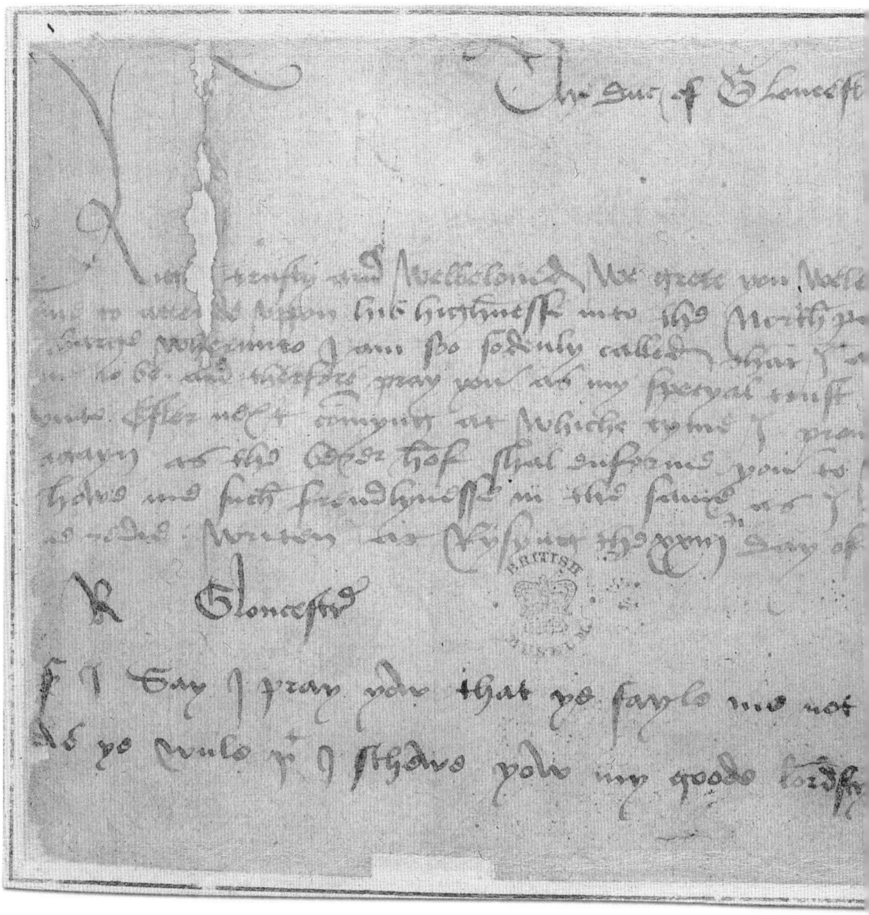

## RICHARD WROTE:

The Duke of Gloucester

Right trusty and wellbeloved, we greet you well. And for as much as the king's good grace has appointed me to attend upon his highness into the north parts of his land, which will be to my great cost and charge, whereunto I am so suddenly called that I am not so well purveyed [provided] of money therefore as behoves [befits] me to be. And therefore pray you, as my special trust is in you, to lend me a hundred pounds of money until Easter next coming at which time I promise you shall be truly thereof content and paid again, as the bearer hereof shall inform you. To whom I pray you give credence therein [ie the bearer could be trusted to take a message back to Richard] and show me such friendliness in the same as I may do for you hereafter, whereunto you shall find me ready. Written at (Castle) Rising, the 24 June (1469)
R Gloucester

## Richard's postscript:

Sir J Say I pray you that you fail me not at this time of my great need as you will that I show you my good lordship in that matter that you labour me for

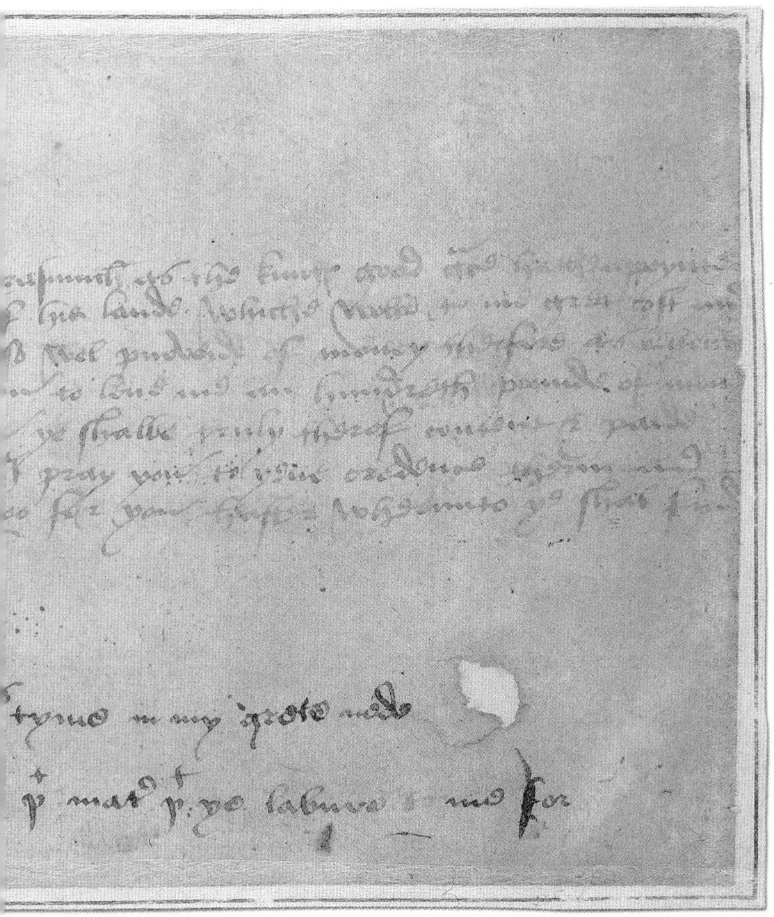

The warring cousins then reached a very uneasy compromise that belied the King's determination to end Warwick's dominance.

Richard was rewarded for his loyalty with the chief military office of Constable of England in October 1469. He was also required to recover the King's authority in the duchy of Lancaster estates of the Welsh marches, which Warwick had absorbed following his execution of William Herbert, Earl of Pembroke, after Edgecote.

March 1470 also saw a revival of Warwick's plotting, and in a remarkable twist of fortune over a six-month period, Edward first drove Warwick and Clarence out of England, but then found himself confronted by an unlikely alliance of his brother, Clarence, Warwick and Henry VI's queen, Margaret. With French help, and the dynastic marriage of his daughter Anne to Edward, Prince of Wales, Warwick again raised his northern supporters. Edward underestimated the strength of support for Warwick, and once Thomas, Lord Stanley – Warwick's brother-in-law – joined the rebels, he and Richard were forced to flee to Holland.

Warwick restored King Henry VI to the throne, while Edward struggled to gather enough support in the Netherlands to launch a recovery of his Crown. In March 1471 his small fleet landed in Yorkshire. Edward and Richard relied on the neutrality of Henry Percy, restored to the earldom of Northumberland the previous year, to reach more friendly territory in the midlands. Then, as Edward's support gathered momentum, Clarence realized the tide was turning against Warwick, and submitted himself to his brother.

On 14 April 1471 the armies of Edward and Warwick met at Barnet. Richard was given his first military command, and acquitted himself with great honour in the mêlée, when many of his retainers

The Battle of Barnet. The Yorkists rallied support on their march south after landing in Yorkshire at the end of March 1471. The Lancastrians holding the capital tried to motivate sympathy for the restored Henry VI, but the citizens allowed Edward's entry on 11 April. Warwick had followed Edward from the midlands and by 12 April his army awaited the King's forces at Barnet. Since Warwick was then allied to his old Lancastrian adversaries Queen Margaret and John, Earl of Oxford, the rebel force was composed of former enemies. This uncertain alliance was undone during the battle. On 14 April, Easter Sunday, the armies fought in heavy fog. Initial Lancastrian successes caused the armies to wheel around, and in the confusion the heraldic badges of Oxford and Edward were mistaken, leading to cries of treason in the Lancastrian force as Oxford's troops were fired upon by their own side. As the Lancastrians began to retreat, Warwick's banner was recognized and he was killed in the rout.

were killed. Warwick also died during the battle. Richard's skill in arms, probably gained under Warwick's tutelage, must have impressed the King, since he was given command of the vanguard that fought decisively against the invading army of Queen Margaret and Edmund Beaufort, Duke of Somerset, at the Battle of Tewkesbury on 4 May. The death in battle of Henry VI's heir Edward, Prince of Wales ended Lancastrian hopes.

**The Battle of Tewkesbury**

This is a late sixteenth-century woodcut depicting the battle. After the victory at Barnet, Edward learned that Margaret of Anjou and her army had landed at Weymouth in Dorset. Edward mustered his forces quickly to prevent the Lancastrians gaining support in the West Country. Following a rapid march, the Lancastrian forces were drawn up with the advantage of the land near Tewkesbury on 4 May. After a Yorkist artillery attack opened the battle, an attempt at a complicated flanking action by the Duke of Somerset failed as Richard, Duke of Gloucester's soldiers fiercely forced the Lancastrians back. Somerset's forces were unsupported and the Lancastrians began to lose heart. Edward steadied his troops and forced the whole enemy army to flee towards Tewkesbury. Edward, Prince of Wales was killed as the Lancastrians were massacred, along with many of the nobles who could have continued the Lancastrian cause.

That Richard had learned how to conduct himself in the hard realities of dynastic civil war is suggested by his role as constable in the swift trial and execution of the Duke of Somerset on 6 May. More seriously for his subsequent reputation, Richard was probably resident in the Tower on the night following the King's return to the capital on 21 May. It was then that Henry VI was put to death.

It is likely that Edward IV ordered Henry's death: few other individuals would have presumed to carry out such an action without the King's agreement. There is no evidence that Richard was present at the murder, but it was a precedent for events in the summer of 1483. As Protector and then King during June of that year, it is most unlikely that Richard was not party to the fate of Edward V and his brother.

Richard's character and personality was formed within a period of shocking civil conflict during which the Yorkist royal family, headed by Edward IV, and its leading kin supporters the Nevilles, headed by Warwick, turned against each other. To his credit, Richard remained steadfastly loyal to his brother during 1469–71, but the vivid demonstration of squabbling and betrayal, murders and summary executions, and the inconstancy of major nobles, must have left a lasting impression on the adolescent Duke. This is the environment in which Richard was introduced to political life.

Tewkesbury Abbey. Some Lancastrian leaders, including the Duke of Somerset, fled into the abbey seeking sanctuary. As it was the nearest church to the battlefield, Edward also entered the abbey to thank God for his victory. His first proclamation of a pardon to his surviving opponents was retracted when the status of the abbey as a sanctuary was disproved. Somerset and several other knights were removed from the abbey and tried and beheaded in Tewkesbury marketplace on 6 May.

edward' rex quart'

# The Prince in the North

## THE HEIR OF WARWICK, 1471–5

Richard of Gloucester's time with the Earl of Warwick before 1469 made him an obvious candidate to take over Warwick's role as royal lieutenant in the north. His previous loyalty meant that a strong regional presence gave Edward a secure foundation in his second reign. Richard had already been made warden of the West March towards Scotland in August 1470, but in the months following Tewkesbury he acquired Warwick's office of chief steward of the northern lands of the duchy of Lancaster, and occupied forfeited Neville estates in Yorkshire and Cumberland.

Portrait of Edward IV. This sixteenth-century copy mirrors that of Richard III (see Preface), and is probably based on a contemporary likeness. Despite his handsome appearance and magnificent court, Edward's reign stagnated after the failed invasion of France in 1475 and the entrenchment of the Queen's influence.

To underline his position as Warwick's successor, Richard married the Earl's daughter Anne Neville at Easter 1472 (his brother Clarence having already married Anne's sister Isabel). Richard also displayed ruthlessness in securing a share of Warwick's personal landed estate, and other family lands that made up the Warwick inheritance. He perhaps emphasized the debt he was owed by the King, contrasting it with Clarence's continued arrogance. Richard had the contacts and experience, but not yet the landed base, from which to run the north on the King's behalf.

The two royal Dukes hotly defended the claims of their Duchesses, even though the northern Neville estates were meant to descend through the male line of that family. In 1475 Edward IV finally agreed to an Act of Parliament that denied the rightful claim of Warwick's nephew and nearest male heir George Neville, Duke of Bedford. Warwick's widow, Anne Beauchamp should also have

Royal Arms of George, Duke of Clarence. Clarence was probably the wealthiest English peer in the mid-1470s. He held an enormous range of lands, and was a skilled and smooth politician. Yet he continued to gamble his influence and his son's inheritance on treasonous behaviour. Clarence's desertion of Edward IV in 1470, and his clashes with Richard over the spoils of the Warwick inheritance, meant that Richard felt little need to intervene to support his brother when he was eventually tried for treason in 1478.

secured most of the Beauchamp, Despenser and Salisbury lands by inheritance and dower, but she was treated as if dead, and the rights passed to her daughters, and thus to their husbands Richard of Gloucester and George of Clarence.

Edward IV seems to have tempered Richard's absorption of the Neville lands by inserting a clause in the Act that allowed Richard and Anne to enjoy them and to pass them to their own male heirs, only for as long as the male heirs of John Neville, Marquis of Montague were alive. This effectively meant George Neville had to marry and produce male children for Richard's own descendants to retain the Neville properties. This was a shaky foundation for a permanent landed base. Richard had cultivated the former Neville servants on a personal basis, but he also needed a more secure footing from which to maintain his national influence (see document 3, *Ties of service*).

While the dispute over the Neville inheritance was ongoing, Richard secured the East Anglian estates of the attainted John de Vere, Earl of Oxford. He also pressurized the exiled Earl's mother Elizabeth into handing over her own lands early in 1473. Richard displayed no scruples in circumventing inheritance laws and using intimidation to secure the range of estates he felt he deserved. By his aggressive replacement of Warwick, Richard also did little to endear himself to other senior northern lords who had hoped to benefit from the Kingmaker's fall.

In 1473 Henry Percy, Earl of Northumberland clashed with Richard over authority in the duchy forest of Knaresborough; by 1474 Northumberland effectively had submitted himself to Richard's service to preserve his own affinity and personal authority from the Duke's forcefulness. The Bishop of Durham, Laurence Booth, also had to surrender Barnard Castle to Richard in 1474, and Lord Stanley's influence in the north-west was certainly not improved by Richard's strengthened position within the duchy lands in the north. All of this was done through the King's direct and often strained influence.

Middleham Castle. Richard's residence there during his formative adolescent years had a strong influence on his life. It remained his main northern residence and the lordship of Middleham provided him with a constant source of support throughout his life. Even after Richard's death, Middleham and Wensleydale families maintained the northern opposition to Henry VII.

# 3 *Ties of service*

Three extracts from a document (in Latin) recording payments of annuities to Richard's supporters in Yorkshire, 1473, just after he was granted the Earl of Warwick's estates at Middleham. Many of these supporters continued to serve Richard up to 1485 (and beyond in some cases). These fees for retaining show Richard moving quickly to secure the loyalty of Warwick's former servants, many of whom were related to each other by marriage, and represented a good proportion of Richmondshire gentry. The Blakeston, Wycliffe and Burgh families were all based in the local area and had long ties of service to the Neville family.

The document also features figures from further afield who drew their fees from the Middleham estate, such as Richard and Roger Conyers who were kinsmen of William Conyers of Marske (identified as 'Robin of Redesdale') who led the Yorkshire rebellion on behalf of Warwick against Edward IV in April 1469. Other loyal followers of Warwick included are Robert Clifford and Thomas Tunstall, both of whom rebelled against Edward IV during 1469–71. Clearly, Richard saw the value of cultivating gentry with Lancastrian sympathies, and by taking them into his service protected them from any repercussions of their opposition to Edward.

Richard continued Warwick's lead in developing the loyalty of a wide group of gentry, and these servants were to sustain Richard's position in northern society and provide him with a solid platform for his seizure of the throne. Richard retained their loyalty: many of these same families were involved in conspiracies against Henry VII after 1485. Although other factors were involved, for Richard's legacy still to have motivated opposition in the north into the Tudor period is a demonstration of the strong ties of service he formed.

## THE DOCUMENT READS:

... And for the fee of Thomas Blakeston of Blakeston, esquire, by reason of his retainer for term of his life by the lord, at 10 marks [a mark was two-thirds of a pound sterling: 10 marks = £6 13s 4d] per annum by letters patent [open document] of the lord, the tenor of which follows in these words: Richard duke of Gloucester, constable and admiral of England to all whom these presents shall come, greeting. Know you that in consideration of the good and acceptable service that our wellbeloved servant Thomas Blakeston of Blakeston, esquire has given and is due to give to us in the future, according to the force, form and effect specified in certain indentures made between us, the aforesaid duke and the said Thomas.

We have granted to the same Thomas an annuity of ten marks sterling to have and take each year during his life proceeding from the issues, profits, and revenues of our lordship of Middleham by the hands of our receiver there for the time being, at the feasts of St Martin in winter and Pentecost by even portions. As proof of which we have caused to be issued these our letters patent. Dated 3 September in the thirteenth year of the reign of Edward the fourth after the conquest of England. That is at terms St Martin and Pentecost within the time of the account and the acquittance [settlement] of the same Thomas was delivered and remains [on file] £6 13s 4d

And for the fee of Robert Wyclyff, esquire, by reason of his retainer for term of his life by the lord, at 20 marks per annum by letters patent of the lord, the tenor of which follows in these words: Richard duke of Gloucester, constable and admiral of England to all whom these presents shall come, greeting. Know you that in consideration of the good and acceptable service that our wellbeloved servant Robert Wyclyff, esquire has given and is due to give to us in the future, according to the force, form and effect specified in certain indentures made between us, the aforesaid duke and the said Robert.

We have granted to the same Robert an annuity of twenty marks sterling to have and take each year during his life proceeding from the issues and revenues of our lordship of Middleham and its members by the hands of our receiver there for the time being, at the feasts of Easter and St Michael by even portions. As proof of which we have caused to be issued these our letters patent. Dated 4 October in the thirteenth year of the reign of Edward the fourth after the conquest of England. That is at terms Easter and St Michael within the time of the account and the acquittance of the same Robert was delivered and remains [on file] £13 6s 8d

And for the fee of Alice Burgh, gentlewoman, in certain special causes and considerations herself granted by the lord for the term of her life at 20 marks per annum by letters patent of the lord, the tenor of which follows in these words: Richard duke of Gloucester, constable and admiral of England to all whom these presents shall come, greeting. Know you that we for certain special causes and considerations moving, and of our certain knowledge and mere motion [Richard's authority to act] grant to our welbeloved Alice Burgh, gentlewoman, an annuity of twenty marks sterling per annum, the same to Alice to have and take for the term of her life from the issues and revenues of our lordship of Middleham in co. York by the hands of our receiver there for the time being, at the feasts of Pentecost and St Martin in winter by even portions. As proof of which we have caused to be issued these our letters patent. Dated 1 March in the thirteenth year of the reign of Edward the fourth after the conquest of England. That is at terms Pentecost and St Martin in winter within the time of the account and the acquittance of the same Alice was delivered and remains [on file] £6 8s 4d

[illegible] per manus receptoris nostri ibidem pro tempore existentis ad festa Sancti Martini in yeme et Pentecostes per equales
porciones. In cuius rei testimonium has litteras nostras fieri fecimus patentes. Datum apud Castrum nostrum de Midelham
xxiiij die Septembris Anno regni Regis Edwardi quarti post conquestum Anglie terciodecimo. Et pro terminis
Sancti Martini et Pentecostes infra tempus compoti ad x li. [illegible] super compotum liberatum.

Et in feodo Thome Blakeston armigeri concessi sibi per eundem dominum ad terminum vite sue ad x marcas per annum per litteras domini
patentes quarum tenor sequitur in hec verba. Ricardus dux Gloucestrie Constabularius et Admirallus Anglie Omnibus ad
quos presentes littere nostre pervenerint salutem. Sciatis quod nos considerantes bonum et acceptabile servicium quod dilectus serviens
noster Thomas Blakeston de Blakeston armiger nobis impendit et impendet iuxta formam cuiusdam in quibusdam
indenturis factis inter nos prefatum ducem et predictum Thomam specificatam imposterum impendere debet et debebit
concessimus eidem Thome quandam annuitatem decem marcarum sterlingorum habendam et annuatim percipiendam eidem Thome
durante vita sua de exitibus proficuis et revencionibus dominii nostri de Midelham per manus receptoris
nostri ibidem pro tempore existentis ad festa Sancti Martini in yeme et Pentecostes per equales porciones. In cuius rei
testimonium has litteras nostras fieri fecimus patentes. Datum xxiiij die Septembris Anno regni Regis Edwardi
quarti post conquestum Anglie terciodecimo. Et pro terminis Sancti Martini et Pentecostes infra tempus compoti
ut [?] ipsius Thome liberatum et cetera. — vj li. xiij s. iiij d.

Et in feodo Roberti Wycliff armigeri concessi sibi per eundem dominum ad terminum vite sue ad xx marcas per annum per litteras
domini patentes quarum tenor sequitur in hec verba. Ricardus dux Gloucestrie Constabularius et Admirallus Anglie
Omnibus ad quos presentes littere nostre pervenerint salutem. Sciatis quod nos considerantes bonum et acceptabile
servicium quod dilectus serviens noster Robertus Wycliff armiger nobis impendit et impendet iuxta formam cuiusdam
in quibusdam indenturis factis inter nos prefatum ducem et predictum Robertum specificatam imposterum impendere
debet et debebit concessimus eidem Roberto quandam annuitatem xx marcarum sterlingorum habendam et annuatim percipiendam
eidem Roberto ad terminum vite sue de exitibus et revencionibus manerii de Midelham in comitatu
Eboraci per manus receptoris ibidem pro tempore existentis ad festa Pasche et Sancti Michaelis per equales porciones.
In cuius rei testimonium has litteras nostras fieri fecimus patentes. Datum iiij die Octobris Anno xj Edwardi
quarti post conquestum Anglie xiij. Et pro terminis Pasche et Sancti Michaelis infra tempus compoti ut
[?] ipsius Roberti super compotum liberatum et cetera. — xiij li. vj s. viij d.

Et in feodo Alexandri Knyght generosi sibi pro diversis et consideracionibus specialibus per dominum concessis ad
terminum vite sue ad xx marcas per annum per litteras domini patentes quarum tenor sequitur in hec verba. Ricardus
dux Gloucestrie Constabularius et Admirallus Anglie Omnibus ad quos presentes littere nostre pervenerint salutem.
Sciatis quod nos ex certis causis et consideracionibus nos specialiter moventibus ac ex certa sciencia et mero
motu nostris concessimus dilecto nobis Alexandro Knyght generoso quandam annuitatem viginti marcarum
sterlingorum habendam et annuatim percipiendam eidem Alexandro ad terminum vite sue de exitibus et revencionibus dominii nostri de Midelham
in comitatu Eboraci per manus receptoris nostri ibidem pro tempore existentis ad festa Pentecostes et Sancti Martini
in yeme per equales porciones. In cuius rei testimonium has litteras nostras fieri fecimus patentes. Datum primo
die mensis Marcii Anno regni Regis Edwardi iiij post conquestum Anglie xiij. Et pro terminis
Pentecostes ~~et Sancti Martini~~ infra tempus compoti ut [?] super compotum liberatum et cetera. — xiij li. vj s. viij d.

Summa [illegible]

Loys par la grace de dieu Roy
de france. Scauoir faiſons
a tous preſens et aduenir.

## POWER WITHOUT RIVAL: RICHARD AT THE HEIGHT OF YORKIST KINGSHIP, 1475–83

The period before 1475, therefore, saw Richard shake off his regional rivals; he was given a free hand by the King to establish his own status as uncrowned lord of the north. There is also evidence that from the mid-decade, Richard adopted a public martial stance to strengthen his bonds with the northern English aristocracy, whose lifestyle was still focused on the military threat from Scotland.

Although his strategic capacities had not really been tested, Richard was clearly a hawk in Edward IV's war camp during the English invasion of France in 1475. He may well have been one of those that agreed with the Duke of Burgundy's rebuke of Edward's acceptance of the truce with Louis XI. Richard would surely have approved of Burgundy's reminder of the honour that previous English kings had generated by fighting for their rights in France.

Louis XI, King of France, depicted in 1476, on the statutes of the Order of St Michael presented to Henry VIII by François I in 1526. Louis established the order in 1469 to rival the English Order of the Garter and the Burgundian Order of the Fleece. Edward IV's failure to fight the French in 1475, and his acceptance of a pension from Louis, have been proposed as causes of renewed faction fighting in England by 1483.

Richard was disappointed that Edward agreed to be 'bought-off', and publicly absented himself from the meeting of the two Kings at Picquigny on 29 August 1475. Similarly, in 1477 the King blocked Richard's intention to send troops to Burgundy to defend his sister Margaret's lands from French attack after the Battle of Nancy. Richard may have felt that the increasingly corpulent Edward was not fulfilling his own potential as monarch, nor enhancing the legacy of their father, who would, no doubt, have behaved very differently towards France had he lived to become king of England.

Richard skilfully galvanized the military demeanour he projected and the support it generated in various campaigns on the Scottish border once the period of Anglo-Scottish truce ended in 1479. He had disagreed with the 1474 Treaty of Edinburgh, and in 1482 launched a full-scale invasion that captured Edinburgh and Berwick from the Scots.

In successfully revitalizing English military prestige on the border, Richard forged a positive national reputation that was magnified many times within the region he dominated. By the beginning of 1483 he was hereditary warden of the West March; Edward IV then offered him a new county palatine, some of which was to be conquered in south-west Scotland. This would have demanded further military campaigning from the northern gentry, and could only have further entrenched Richard's ruling position.

Anthony Woodville, Earl Rivers presenting his translation of the *Dictes and Sayings of the Philosophers* to Edward IV, Queen Elizabeth and Edward, Prince of Wales, in the Star Chamber at Westminster in 1477. This was the first book to be printed in England. Richard may be the other royal figure dressed in blue and ermine.

During the final years of Edward IV's reign, therefore, Richard consolidated his regional position in largely harmonious political circumstances. Land exchanges concentrated his estates in Yorkshire; he spent much more time at his residences and seldom ventured south following the judicial murder of Clarence in 1478. Richard used this time to develop religious patronage – founding collegiate chapels at Middleham and Barnard Castle and supporting Coverham Abbey in Wensleydale.

Richard III's Court of Common Pleas Great Seal (see the entire document pp. 72–3). This is the obverse showing the King enthroned in his coronation robes, with the sceptre, orb and crown – the most potent symbols of a king anointed by God.

After 1476 he also developed a foothold in the palatinate of Durham, through the sympathetic episcopate of Bishop William Dudley. In a series of skilful political manoeuvres, Richard made himself the welcome and benevolent patron of northern towns. The citizens of York, especially, considered him to be their good lord. The Duke also brought an impartiality to the dispensation of justice. In arbitrating disputes, he famously found against his own servants on a number of occasions and enhanced his reputation by providing a means of redress for the poor of the region through his council. This was institutionalized as the Council of the North during his reign.

Much of this continued at the same time as he ruthlessly pursued his personal interests, so there was a degree of smooth public relations in such measures. But this was no more than that displayed by all other lords with their own sphere of influence to preserve. It also is a good example of the interchangeable public and private aspects of noble lordship at the end of the fifteenth century. Only good lords confident of their personal power could afford to display such public benevolence.

# Prince, Protector and King

## THE STRUGGLE FOR CONTROL, APRIL–MAY 1483

Richard was but one of many powerful nobles given distinct regional authority by Edward IV. While Edward was alive this was a well-managed system. If rivalries did emerge – as between Edward's right-hand man William, Lord Hastings, and the Queen's son by her first marriage Thomas Grey, Marquis of Dorset – the King was able to contain them through his personal intervention. With Edward's sudden death on 9 April 1483, however, all major figures must have contemplated the security of their position and power, and several lords aligned themselves to benefit from the patronage of his successor.

King Richard and Queen Anne in coronation regalia with their personal heraldry blazoned on their garments. Anne was a sixteen-year-old widow when she married Richard in 1472, but although she and Richard spent most of their short adult lives together, little is known of their marriage.

Their grief at their son's death was 'almost bordering on madness', and they did share common religious interests in the north during the 1470s. The premature deaths of both Anne and Richard in 1485 prevented the creation of evidence that might offer more insight into their personal lives together.

Edward, Prince of Wales – Edward V – was at Ludlow when his father died. His household and Council were dominated by Anthony Woodville (Earl Rivers) and other members of the Queen's family. Richard had no history of conflict with the Woodvilles, but it is likely that an under-age King, dominated by the Queen's upwardly mobile blood relatives, would have pursued a different agenda to that seen in the stable last years of Edward IV. Certainly, Richard no longer had guarantees about his north-western palatinate, nor even that his northern dominance was necessary or acceptable.

Evidence of Richard's unease with, or disapproval of, Edward IV's regime is minimal. Although Edward needed to maintain the strong and loyal lordship of his brother, he was complicit in most of Richard's more dubious actions, and can only have expected that the Duke would support the accession of Prince Edward. In reality, Richard was crowned King within twelve weeks of Edward IV's death, to the complete astonishment of contemporaries.

In the first days after his brother's death, Richard very properly swore an oath of allegiance to Edward V, but at the same time he also made contact with Lord Hastings and Henry Stafford, Duke of Buckingham. Hastings's history of animosity towards Elizabeth Woodville's son, the Marquis of Dorset, made him wary of his place in the minority regime. Buckingham, who had been excluded from all authority by Edward IV, perhaps saw the opportunity of a role more suited to his royal status, a fact possibly recognized by Richard also.

Map of Ludlow, 1570s. From the 1460s into the sixteenth century, Ludlow was the principal residence of the Prince of Wales. It was here that the Prince's Council administered the March counties on behalf of the Crown. Edward IV's son, Edward, and Henry VII's heir, Arthur, resided here and began to master the political skills needed for their future reigns. Unfortunately, neither these two Princes, nor Richard III's son Edward, lived to inherit the Crown.

There can be no suggestion at this stage of a conspiracy against Edward V. Rather, the confederation of these nobles was probably a move to delay Edward's coronation, since such a ceremony in April 1483 may have left the three lords isolated, making it difficult to gain footholds in the Woodville-dominated household and council that would surely have followed.

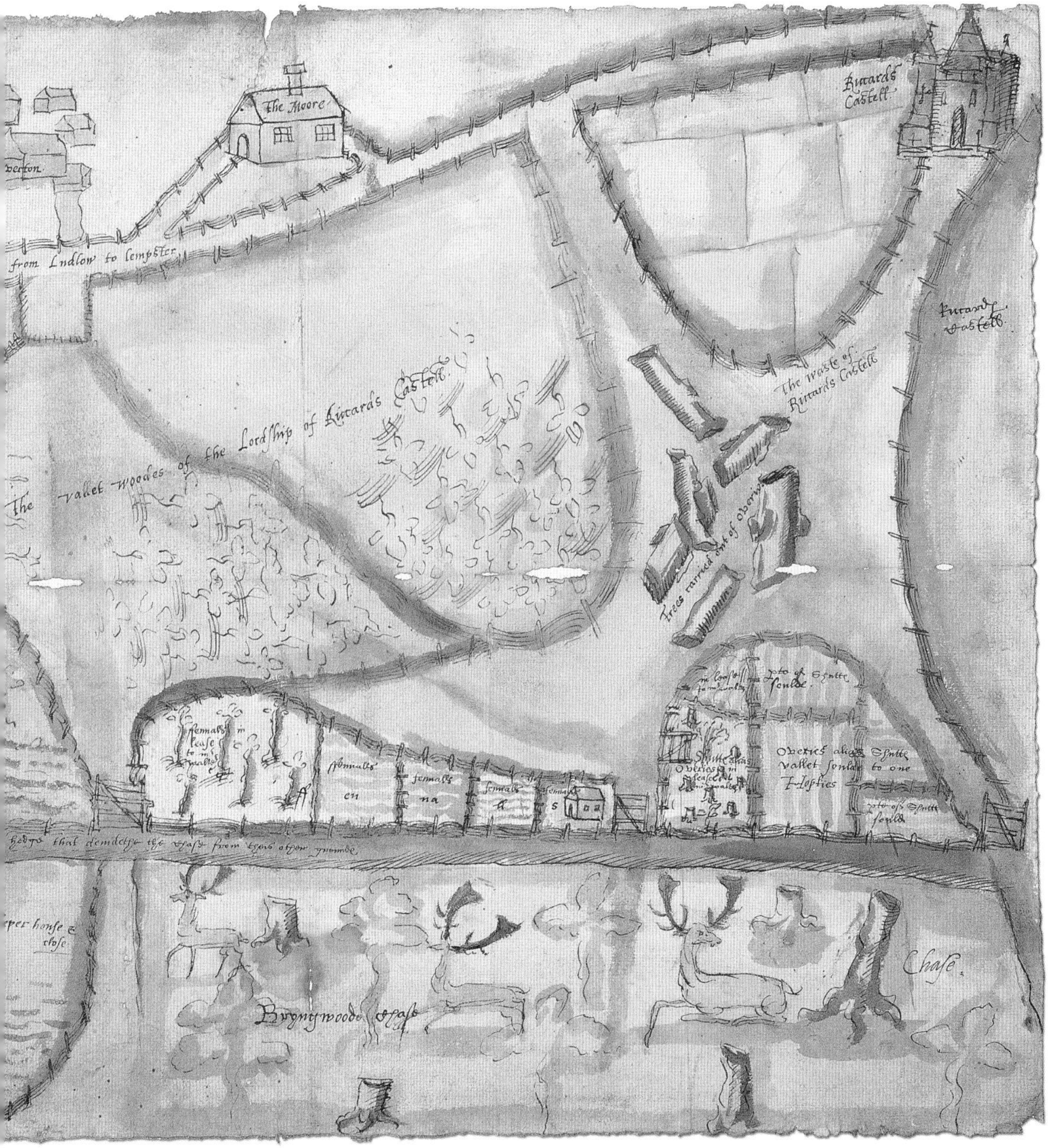

The three lords argued for a protectorate – allegedly promised to Richard by the dying Edward IV – but a compromise was reached in the royal Council whereby Richard, as the most experienced and senior relative of the new King, would head his Council, with the coronation at the start of May.

Government business continued as normal, but at some point during the final ten days of April 1483, Richard, Buckingham and Hastings decided to act against the Woodvilles and to secure the person of Edward V. This move may be seen as a final attempt to avert a Woodville dominated regime, while at the same time ensuring Richard's pre-eminence as Protector.

On 30 April 1483 Buckingham and Richard arrested Earl Rivers, his nephew Sir Richard Grey, and Sir Thomas Vaughan, chamberlain of Edward V's household, as they journeyed with King Edward through Northamptonshire towards London. Richard alleged that the Woodvilles planned to remove him (Richard) from power by killing him.

Edward V, depicted on a stained glass window in the church of St Matthew, Coldridge, Devon. Much like Edward VI, in the 1540s, the teenage Prince Edward showed encouraging signs of fulfilling the dynastic hopes of his father. Edward was educated with the knowledge and practical skills needed to maintain the Yorkist dynasty on the throne. He generated the loyalty of many leading politicians of the 1470s, and not just because they had a vested interest in his success. Although he was dominated by the Woodville group, there are suggestions that Edward V would have developed strong authority in his own right.

The *Hastings Hours*: the Flight into Egypt. In common with all major political figures of the late fifteenth century, Lord Hastings was a cultured man at ease both in the library and on the battlefield. His honourable defence of Edward V's interests has made him a tragic victim of Richard's coup.

The King had little choice but to accept these charges, since he had already been persuaded to travel with a small military presence, in case citizens became alarmed at a large force descending on London. Rivers, although a wily politician, was completely outmanoeuvred.

In dismay at this coup, Elizabeth Woodville sought sanctuary in Westminster Abbey with her daughters and younger son, the Duke of York. Hastings pacified the capital in preparation for the King's arrival, and with the swift removal of the short-term Woodville threat, Richard became the unchallenged Protector of the young King, with Edward IV's leading supporter, Lord Hastings, as the guarantor of his good faith towards Edward V. Read an eyewitness account of events at this time: document 4, ***News from London.***

The establishment of the King's authority could, and perhaps should then have progressed smoothly. The three allied lords had outwitted the Woodvilles and revealed the weaknesses of their recently created power. A short protectorate would have led to Edward's coronation and full authority at the age of twelve, under the guidance of a balanced Council.

However, the King had spent much of his short life in the company of his mother and her family, and was likely to demand for them some ceremonial role at the coronation, and wider political responsibilities once he was crowned. Richard had made determined enemies of the Woodvilles, and his actions had also potentially opened a Pandora's box of enmity and conflict that Edward IV had previously contained.

# 4 *News from London*

This is the first of two letters (in English) from Simon Stallworth to Sir William Stoner, recounting events in London; this one is dated 9 June 1483 (see also document 6, ***Much trouble and doubt***).

Sir William Stoner was a leading gentry figure in Oxfordshire and Berkshire. He rebelled against Richard in October 1483 and forfeited his estates and influence. Simon Stallworth was, effectively, Stoner's business agent in London and at court. This type of newsletter between servant and master was a common way of transmitting information on major events. Yet out of all the private correspondence that must have been created, this is one of only three letters to have survived which shed any light on how unfolding news was received in the capital during June 1483 (see also documents 5 and 6).

This first letter suggests interest and concern at events, but seems calmly confident that things are under control, since there is nothing new to report. Although the Queen and Duke of York are still in sanctuary, Richard and Buckingham have maintained the business of the Council. Plans are underway for the coronation, and Edward V is visibly receiving visitors, such as the Duchess of Gloucester, in his Tower apartments. Stoner will be travelling up to Westminster for the coronation, when he shall learn more detail for himself. Stallworth even has time to pass on detailed information from Richard himself concerning the fine for a foreigner ('Edward Johnson of Thame') seeking denization as an English subject.

Clearly, Stallworth was unaware that Richard's governmental diligence and attention to detail disguised feverish preparations for his coup. The following day, Sir Richard Ratcliffe (one of Richard's closest allies) was dispatched on a secret mission to the north, to request troops from the authorities in York, on Richard's behalf. Richard needed backing to confront the Queen's family, who, he alleged, intended to destroy the old nobility of the realm and to disinherit the men of property in areas where Richard was dominant. Four days after this letter was written, Richard executed Lord Hastings and moved to take the throne.

## SIMON STALLWORTH WROTE:

Master Stoner, After due recommendations, I recommend me to you. As for tidings since I wrote to you, we hear none new. The queen keeps still at Westminster my lord of York; my lord of Salisbury [Bishop of Salisbury] with others more, will not depart as yet. Wheresoever can be found any goods of my lord Marquis, it is taken [the Marquis of Dorset's lands and goods had been confiscated]. The prior of Westminster was and yet is in a great trouble for certain goods delivered to him by my lord Marquis. My lord Protector, my lord of Buckingham with all other lords as well temporal as spiritual were at Westminster in the council chamber from 10am to 2pm, but there was none that spoke with the queen. There is great business against the coronation which shall be this day fortnight, as we say, when I trust you will be at London, then shall you know all the world. The king is at the Tower; your lady of Gloucester came to London on Thursday last. Also my lord [Richard] commends himself to you and gave me in commandment to write to you and prays you to be a good master to Edward Johnson of Thame he was with my lord and sued to be made a denizen for fear of the payment of his subsidy, and my lord sent to Jeves the clerk of the crown and saw the commission and showed to him that he should pay but 6s 8d for himself, and so were he better to do than to be made denizen, which would cost him the third part of his goods. And as for such as have troubled [caused trouble] within the lordship of Thame, my lord will be advised by you at your coming for the reformation, if you take note or you come, for he thinks that they shall be punished in example of others. And Jesus preserve you, in haste from London by the hands of your servant the 9th day of June.

Simon Stallworth

Wurschypfull syr aftyr all recomendacion I recomaunde me to yowe. As for tydyngs syns I
wrote to yowe we hav non newe. ye Quene kepys stylle Westm' my lord of Yorke my
lord of Salysbury wt othyr mo wyche wyll nott departe as yytt. Wher so ever kan
be founde any godys of my lord Marques it is tayne. ye Prior of Westm' was
& yitt is in a gret trobyll for sertyne godys delyveryd to hyme by my lord Marques.
my lord Protectour my lord of Bukyngham wt all othyr lordys as wele temporale as spirituale
wer at Westm' in ye councelchamber fro x to ij butt ther was none yt spake wt ye Quene.
Ther is gret besyness ageyns ye coronacione wyche schalbe yis day fortnyght as we say.
When I trust ye wylbe at London & ye schall here all ye worlde. ye Kyng is at
ye Towre. My lady of Glocestre come to London on Thorsday last. Also my lord
comendys hyme to yowe & he gave me in commaundment to wryte to yowe & pray yowe to be
good mayster to Edward Johnson of Thame. He was wt my lord & desyryd to be made a
Denysen for fer of ye paymentt of ye subsedy & my lord send to Hobbe ye clerke of
ye Crowne & take ye commissione & schewyd to hyme yt if he schuld pay butt ye custum
for hym ~~sef~~ selfe & so was he nott to do ye to be made Denysen wyche
wolde coste hym ye thyrd parte of hys good. & as for suche as hav robbyth te
in ye lordschyppe of Thame my lord wylbe advysyd by yowe at yor comyng for ye reformacion
yf ye take mo or ye come. for he thynkys yt yei schalbe punysshed in ensample of
othyr & Jesu preserve yowe. in hast from London by ye handys of yowr frende

ye ix day of June

Simon Stallworthe.

With Rivers, Grey and Vaughan imprisoned in the north, and Woodville power scattered but not broken, all Richard had achieved was to place himself most prominently in Edward V's government. The problem of how to include the Woodvilles without risking his own position under the new King still remained; as did the difficulty of constituting a functioning ruling council until the King came of age, possibly at sixteen in November 1486 – at least three years in the future.

Rubbing of a memorial brass to Sir Thomas Vaughan, from Westminster Abbey. As treasurer of the chamber to Edward V as Prince of Wales, Vaughan was staunchly loyal to his royal master. He rose to prominence through close links to the Woodvilles, and this meant that in May 1483 he was targeted as a likely opponent of Richard's course of action.

## SEIZING THE CROWN, JUNE 1483

During May 1483, Richard began his next phase of action. In this we can see for the first time evidence that he sought the Crown. Having succeeded in deflating Woodville power, Hastings may have been quite happy that his own and Richard's influence would counter-balance any Woodville involvement within Edward V's regime. However, Richard's personal situation required further action, since George Neville, Duke of Bedford had died on 4 May 1483 without marriage or children.

Richard's interest in the northern Neville lands would now end at his death, and his son Edward, who was probably aged eight at this time, would inherit no ready-made power base. Having spent more than a decade developing a long-term strategy for his dominance of the north, Richard now needed to hold onto power at the centre at least long enough to force through legislation that secured his title to the Neville lands.

With the hostility of the Woodvilles now guaranteed, there was little prospect that this could be achieved without a vicious and protracted struggle. Richard may therefore have decided that a more ruthless and dynamic course of action was necessary to preserve his influence. This change of behaviour caused confusion in London (see document 5, ***Rumour in the realm***).

On 7 May a meeting of Edward IV's executors was held at Baynards Castle, the London home of Richard's mother Cecily Neville. Those present became reluctant to prove the will, and Edward's seals and jewels were confiscated. The executors included Lords Stanley and Hastings, and Bishop Morton of Ely, who could simply have been waiting for more secure times before putting Edward IV's legacy into effect.

However, Richard and Buckingham, also present, may have been forcing an alternative issue. Given the business under discussion, this meeting was possibly the first semi-public indication that Richard had been investigating the illegitimacy of Edward IV or of his sons.

The meeting seems also to mark the beginning of a cooling of Richard's relationship with Hastings, since it would have been apparent that Richard was contemplating something more than a decisive blow against the Woodvilles. It is perhaps no coincidence that Hastings soon after began to associate more closely with those on the margins of Richard's trust, such as Stanley and Morton.

Richard ordered soldiers from the north on 10 June to protect him from an apparent renewal of Woodville plotting. Their depleted resources made this an unlikely possibility. More probably, Richard needed military backing for the action he was planning.

# 5 *Rumour in the realm*

The wool merchant George Cely scribbled this highy confused note in London in June 1483. It must have been written between 13 and 26 June, since Hastings is dead, but Richard is not yet King. London was rife with rumour, and Cely attempted to categorize what he had heard into items of news that were likely to be true, and those that were considered fears without further basis.

The note is a mixture of possibilities (the Scottish invasion) with the bleakest rumours (the King has been killed), and the misinformation that Richard and Buckingham themselves created (that Richard himself is in peril from the Woodvilles). Of the four 'facts' – a Scottish invasion; the death of Hastings; the death of John Morton, Bishop of Ely; and danger to Thomas Rotherham, the Chancellor – only the death of Hastings was true. The fears circulating at the time were that Edward V was dead; Richard was in danger; the Duke of York was in jeopardy; and that the Earl of Northumberland and John Lord Howard were dead. The last line refers to Sir John Weston, prior of the Order of St John of Jerusalem, who was Cely's main source of information.

As a merchant of the staple, Cely was well connected and experienced in the effect of events on trade. We can presume that he discovered the accuracy of his facts and rumours fairly quickly. However, the fact that he could not obtain accurate information on events that were developing around him only heightens the sense that the smokescreen created by Richard and Buckingham was having its intended effect. Deliberate misinformation at the time makes it much harder to see things clearly over five hundred years later.

## GEORGE CELY WROTE:

There is great rumour in the realm. The Scots have done great in England. The Chamberlain [Lord Hastings] is deceased, in trouble [danger] the Chancellor is disproved [discredited] and not content. The bishop of Ely is dead. If the king, God save his life, were deceased. The duke of Gloucester were in any peril. If my lord Prince were, God defend, were troubled. If my lord Northumberland were dead or greatly troubled. If my lord Howard were slain. *De monsieur* St John's

Ther ys grett romber in the reme / the Scottes has done grett
yn ynglond / schamberlayne ys dessesset in trobell the chavnse-
ler ys dessprowett and nott content / the bysschoppe of Ely ys dede
yff the kynge god save hys lyffe wher dessesset / the dewke of glo-
setter wher in any peryll / yffe my lord prynsse wher god
defend wher trobellett / yf my lord of northehomberlond
wher dede or grettly trobellytt / yf my lord haward wher
slayne

De movnsewr Saint Jonys

At a carefully managed Council meeting on Friday 13 June, Richard accused Hastings, Stanley, Morton and the Archbishop of York of plotting treason against him. Hastings was immediately and brutally beheaded on Tower Green and the other lords imprisoned, although Stanley narrowly avoided death in the struggle. Read Simon Stallworth's contemporary account of these events: document 6, ***Much trouble and doubt.***

On the following Monday Richard's troops surrounded the sanctuary at Westminster and Thomas Bourchier, Archbishop of Canterbury was called upon to persuade Elizabeth Woodville to surrender Richard, Duke of York. As a result, he joined his brother in the Tower, Parliament was cancelled and Edward V's coronation again postponed.

A view of Pontefract Castle in the 1570s. Pontefract was the centre of duchy of Lancaster administration in Yorkshire. It was also a major royal castle and was the muster point for several northern armies during the late fifteenth century. It was during one such muster, immediately before Richard's seizure of the Crown, that the Earl of Northumberland oversaw the execution, perhaps after a cursory trial, of Rivers, Grey and Vaughan.

After a further week of planning, on 22 June Richard's claim to the throne as the only true heir of his father Richard, Duke of York, was publicly proclaimed during a sermon by Ralph Shaw at St Paul's Cross. This alleged firstly that Edward IV was conceived in adultery and that therefore he and all his children were bastards. This was later changed to a declaration that Edward's marriage of 1464 was invalid because of an existing pre-contract to the Earl of Shrewsbury's daughter, Eleanor Butler. This too meant that under Church law the children of Edward and Elizabeth were illegitimate and should not inherit the Crown.

On 24 June, Buckingham made a similar pronouncement at a gathering of London officials at the Guildhall, and over the following two days delegations of gentry petitioned Richard at Baynards Castle to take the Crown. With troops mustering under the Earl of Northumberland in the north, Richard

# 6 *Much trouble and doubt*

This is Simon Stallworth's second letter (in English) to Sir William Stoner, dated 21 June 1483. In the aftermath of Hastings's execution, Stallworth's tone has changed completely. There is no time for private business matters, and all news reports events and speculation about how things may unfold. The style is more concerned, since Richard's action against Hastings and the presence of armed men at Westminster were causing anxiety around the city.

Stallworth reports that the Duke of York has been taken from Westminster to the Tower – presumably he is 'merry' because he is joining his brother Edward V. There is a hint that Richard's information about a Woodville plot has been circulated widely, since the prospect of 20,000 men descending on London is expected solely to keep the peace (this was a great exaggeration but indicates the extent to which Richard's allegations of a major Woodville plot were accepted). The arrest of Morton (Bishop of Ely) and Archbishop Rotherham (Archbishop of York) at the Council meeting of 13 June is still effective. The detention of Hastings's former mistress, Elizabeth Shore, and of Oliver King, Edward IV's former secretary, is also commented upon. John Foster was a servant of the Queen who had carried news to her son, the Marquis of Dorset, in sanctuary.

The cryptic postscript about the servants of Hastings transferring their allegiance to Buckingham has also not been confirmed from other documents. It is, however, a suggestion that politically astute gentry lost no time in adjusting their positions to changing events. There is clearly no awareness in Stallworth's letter that Richard was about to take the throne, which occurred within the week.

During the mid-1970s a historical debate developed over this letter and the dating of Hastings's death. New material from the Mercers' Company archives was interpreted to suggest that Hastings was killed on Friday 20 June ('Friday last' as this letter suggests). However, the change in handwriting at the word 'Protector's', suggests that the letter was completed in Stallworth's own hand on Saturday 21 June after a period of sickness, to which he refers at the end. The scored through sentence may also have been crossed out when Stallworth completed the letter, following new information on the rapidly changing course of events.

## SIMON STALLWORTH WROTE:

Worshipful Sir, I commend me to you, and for tidings, I hold you happy that you are out of the press [i.e. in the 'thick of it'], for with us is much trouble and every man doubts another. As on Friday last was the Lord Chamberlain [Lord Hastings] beheaded soon upon noon. On Monday last was at Westminster great plenty of harnessed men [soldiers in body armour]. There was the deliverance of the duke of York to my lord Cardinal, my lord Chancellor, and other many lords temporal; and with him met my lord of Buckingham in the middle of the hall of Westminster; my lord Protector [Richard] receiving him at the Star Chamber door with many loving words; and so [he] departed with my lord Cardinal to the Tower where he is, blessed be Jesus, merry [happy]. The Lord Lisle [Edward Grey] is come to my lord Protector and waits upon him. It is thought there shall be 20,000 of my lord Protector and my lord of Buckingham's men in London this week, to what intent I know not, but to keep the peace. My lord [Richard] has much business and more than he is content withal [as well], if any other ways would be taken. The lord Archbishop of York [and] the bishop of Ely are yet in the Tower, with master Oliver King ~~I suppose they shall come out nevertheless~~. There are men in their places for sure keeping. And I suppose that there shall be sent men of my lord Protector's to these lords places in the country. They are not likely to come out of ward [custody] yet. As for Foster, he is in hold and many fear for his life. Mistress Shore is in prison; what shall happen [to] her I know not. I pray you pardon me of more writing – I am so sick that I may not well hold my pen. And Jesus preserve you. From London the 21st day of June [1483] by the hands of your servant

Simon Stallworth

All the lord Chamberlain's men become my lord of Buckingham's men

Worschipfull Sir I comend me to you And for tydyngs I hold you happy that ye ar oute of the prese for w^t
huse is myche trobull and euery mann dowtes other. As on fryday last was the lord Chamberleyn hedded sone apon
noon. on monday last was at Westm' gret plenty of harnest men ther was the dylyueraunce of the Duke
of yorke to my lord Cardenale my lord Chaunceler and other many lordes Temporale And w^t hym mett my lord of
Bukyngham in the myddes of the hall of Westm'. my lord protectour recevynge hyme at the Starre Chamber
Dore with many lovynge wordys and so departed w^t my lord Cardenale to the toure wher he is blessid
be Jhesu mery. The lord Lisle is come to my lord protectour And awaites apon hyme. yt is thougth ther
schalbe xx thousand of my lord protectour and my lord of Bukyngham men in London this weke to what
intent I knowe note but to kep the peas. my lord hath myche besynes and more then he is content w^t all.
if any other ways wold be tane the lord Archebysshop of yorke the Bysshop of Ely ar yet in the towre
w^t Master Olyuer Kynge ~~I suppose they schall come oute neuerthelesse~~ Ther ar men in ther placys for sure
kepynge And I suppose that ther schall be sent menn of my lord protectour to thes lordes placys
in the countre they ar not lyke to come oute of ward yett. As for Foster he is
in hold and menn fere hys lyffe. Mastres Chore is in prisone what schall happyn
hyr I knowe nott I pray you pardone me of more wrytynge I ame so seke that
I may nott well hold my penne And Jhesu preserue you from London the xxi day of
June by the hande of your seruaunt

Symon Stallworthe

All the lord Chamberleyne mene be come
my lordes of Bokynghame menn

ordered the execution of Rivers, Grey and Vaughan on 25 June. The next day, after a further submission by the Lords and Commons, he occupied the King's chair in the court of King's Bench in Westminster Hall. Richard was King as the rightful heir of the Yorkist dynasty.

## THE PRINCES IN THE TOWER

The fate of Edward V and Richard, Duke of York was just as much a mystery in 1483 as it is today. Towards the end of June their personal servants were dismissed. Dr John Argentine, the young King's physician, gave an eyewitness account of his last time with Edward, but knew nothing more of his whereabouts. By the middle of July, commentators reported that the boys were withdrawn to the private apartments of the Tower. They were never seen again.

Only one English source has been discovered that offers a specific date for their death before Richard was crowned. The Anlaby family cartulary cited 22 June as the date that Edward V died. Some foreign sources do claim that the Princes were dead before 26 June, and both George Cely's note and Dominic Mancini's account of the situation in London before mid-July suggest similar confused suspicions among London citizens. Document 7, ***Evidence of the Princes' fate?*** may hold a clue as to what happened to the younger Prince.

As is still the case, nothing definite could be discovered of their fate. All of the evidence of Richard's involvement in their deaths is certainly circumstantial. But by not demonstrating publicly that they were either alive, or, through the trial of some scapegoat, killed without his knowledge, Richard fuelled speculation that he was aware of, and responsible for, their deaths.

Two skeletons found in the Tower in 1674 and examined in 1933 may be the bones of the Princes. There have been calls for comparison with DNA from Edward IV's body at Windsor, and this might well prove that the bones are those of Edward V and Richard of York. Since we expect the Princes to have been murdered and buried in the Tower, such a result may come as no surprise. It will certainly not tell us how they died, nor who was responsible.

Because the account of the disappearance of the Princes is so emotive, it has generated many amazing stories of alternative candidates for their murder, and of their miraculous escape and secret survival into the Tudor period. Such tales are often ingenious and entertaining as exercises in speculation, but much of the evidence does not stand up to scrutiny.

The most telling indication of a belief in the Princes' death is Elizabeth Woodville's accommodation with Richard III after March 1484. Guarantees about the safety of her daughters, especially Elizabeth of York, suggest that the former queen was convinced that her sons were dead. Elizabeth also successfully plotted with Margaret Beaufort on behalf of Henry Tudor at the same time, indicating that she was convinced that her own security lay in a Tudor dynasty established on Elizabeth of York's rights as eldest surviving heir of Edward IV.

The Tower of London. By Edward IV's reign, the Tower had been surpassed as a royal residence by newer building work at the palaces of Greenwich, Westminster and Sheen. Yet it remained the key fortress and major armoury of the realm, and its role as the main royal political prison was already long established. Shakespeare's dramatic image of the Princes' fear at their enforced residence there was most probably true in reality.

# 7 *Evidence of the Princes' fate?*

Charter (in Latin) recording the grant of the title of Duke of Norfolk to John, Lord Howard, 28 June 1483. Howard was also made Earl Marshal later the same day, although he is already described as such in this grant.

The dukedom of Norfolk was one of the titles granted in 1477 to Edward IV's youngest son Richard of Shrewsbury, Duke of York, in anticipation of his marriage to Anne, heiress of John Mowbray, Duke of Norfolk, which occurred in January 1478. For Howard to have been granted this title on 28 June 1483, Richard, Duke of York would either have to have been considered dead, legally dead, or else Richard III viewed Edward's award as invalid because York was by then proclaimed illegitimate.

Parliament had not then met to renounce previous gifts with an Act of Resumption, nor had any recognized authority, such as the royal Council, annulled the grant. The promotion of Howard is possible confirmation that the Princes in the Tower were dead, or that there was an intention to kill them, before Richard was crowned. There was also a precedent directly relevant to Richard. In February 1478 his son Edward was granted the earldom of Salisbury, one of Clarence's titles, three days before the execution of the Duke within the Tower.

The charter was an unusual method to record such a grant. It was probably to emphasize broad consent, that Richard chose a format which not only endorsed the award, but also broadcast widely his entitlement to make peerage creations that affected the precedence of noble society.

A further unusual aspect was the language used in this creation. Most documents creating new titles mentioned the diligent service, loyalty, nearness of blood, etc., of the recipient. The grant to Howard is conspicuous for its rhetoric. Richard, having been appointed by God as a man most suited to be king, puts himself in God's place to elevate those whom the common weal have deemed worthy of higher nobility. Despite his abilities, Howard was promoted mainly because he was a close ally of Richard, and vital to the strength of his regime.

## THE CHARTER READS:

The king to the archbishops &c, Whereas the radiance of the eternal king through whom all kings reign and princes have dominion, the ray of his light and glory, in many and divers ways shines upon all his creatures and marks out those who share in his goodness, and whereas We, who under his providential design rule and govern his people, endeavour by his grace to conform our will and acts to his will, we have deemed it right [and] consider it fit by natural and prudent reason to walk in his ways and, insofar as it is granted to us from above, to mark his footsteps, therefore, led by his example, we have determined by the grace and liberality of our royal majesty to illumine [honour] those noble and distinguished men who are most deserving of the public weal [esteem], and hence we have determined to raise the outstanding nobility of our most dear cousin John Howard ....to the higher degree of honour [etc] ...

**The grant then goes on to make Howard Duke of Norfolk, by girding him with the sword, and putting on the cap and golden circlet and delivery of the golden rod**

... The said title and dignity is to be held by him and his heirs male of his body; with further gift to him and his said heirs of £40 out of the farms and issues of the counties of Norfolk and Suffolk to be received at the hands of the sheriff of those counties, &c. By the king, Westminster 28 June 1483.

De creacione Comitis de Notyngham

vacat quia aliter inferius

(9.)

Ricardus dei gracia Rex Anglie et Francie et Dominus Hibernie Archiepiscopis Episcopis Abbatibus Prioribus Ducibus Comitibus Baronibus Justiciariis Vicecomitibus Prepositis Ministris et omnibus Ballivis et fidelibus suis salutem. Sciatis quod nos maiorum strenuitatem ac morum probitatem necnon scienciam fidelitatem et industriam quibus viget emicat atque pollet predilectus et fidelis consanguineus noster Willelmus Vicecomes Berkeley dominus de Berkeley intime ponderantes volentes eundem Willelmum iuxta suorum exigentiam meritorum aliqualiter premiare de gracia nostra speciali ac ex certa sciencia et mero motu nostris ipsum Willelmum in Comitem Notyngham ereximus prefecimus et creavimus et ei nomen statum titulum stilum sedem prerogativam et preeminentiam status illi quomodolibet pertinentes eidem Willelmo damus conferimus et concedimus per presentes Et quia crescente status celsitudine ex consequenti necessario crescunt sumptus et onera grandiora de gracia nostra predicta premissorum intuitu et pro huiusmodi statu decencius et honorificencius per ipsum Willelmum et heredes suos masculos manutenendo et sustentando concessimus eidem Willelmo viginti libras percipiendas annuatim de exitibus proficuis et revencionibus de Com Notyngham et Derb provenientibus per manus vicecomitis eorundem Com pro tempore existentis ad terminos sancti Michaelis Archangeli et Pasche per equales porciones Habendum et tenendum omnia huiusmodi nomen statum titulum stilum sedem prerogativam et preeminentiam cum omnibus suis iuribus et pertinentiis quibuscumque necnon predictas viginti libras annuas eidem Willelmo et heredibus suis masculis de corpore suo legitime procreatis Eo quod expressa mencio de aliis donis sive concessionibus per nos eidem Willelmo ante hec tempora factis in presentibus minime facta existit aut aliquo statuto actu vel ordinacione in contrarium facta sive ordinata non obstante. Hiis testibus venerabilibus patribus Th. Cardinali Archiepiscopo Cantuar Th. London R. Bathon et Wellen et J. Lincoln Cancellario Anglie Episcopis Henrico Buk et Johanne Suff Ducibus Willelmo Arundell et Henrico Northumbr Comitibus Johanne Dudley de Dudley milite et Thoma Stanley de Stanley milite et aliis. Dat per manum nostram apud Westm vicesimo octavo die Junii Anno regni nostri primo.

per ipsum Regem et de dat predicta auctoritate parliamenti

De creacione Ducis Norff

(8.)

R. Archiepiscopis etc salutem. Cum eterni Regis per quem omnes Reges regnant et principes dominantur radius sue lucis et glorie multis variis que modis omnes creaturas suas illuminet bonitatis que sue participes efficiat Nos qui sub eius prudencia et disposicione ipsum regimen et gubernacionem voluntatem et actus nostros voluntati sue conformiter ipsius gracia assistente intendamus dignum duximus omni iuri naturali et politici consentaneum arbitramur nos in viis eius ambulare et in quantum nobis desuper datum est vestigiis eius inherere Atque exemplo eius adducti nobiles et claros viros qui de re publica optime meriti sunt gracia et liberalitate regie magestatis nostre ornare decrevimus Proinde egregiam nobilitatem carissimi consanguinei nostri Johannis Haward Comitis Marescalli Anglie ex nobili prosapia clarissimorum et illustrium virorum ducum Norff procreati veri et indubitati heredis Thome nuper et ultimi Ducis Norff ac eciam gratissima obsequia nobis tam tempore pacis quam belli multipliciter impensa ipsius que eximias atque laudatissimas virtutes assidua meditacione perpendentes ipsum consanguineum nostrum ad altiorem honoris gradum sublimare et erigere decrevimus Unde de gracia nostra speciali ac ex certa sciencia et mero motu nostris dictum consanguineum nostrum in Ducem Norff ereximus creavimus insignivimus prefecimus et ordinavimus ac nomen titulum statum stilum honorem auctoritatem et dignitatem Ducis Norff eidem consanguineo nostro damus et concedimus per presentes ac eum de nomine illo cum titulo statu stilo honore auctoritate et dignitate ceteris que honoribus eidem appendentibus et annexis per gladii cincturam cappe et circuli aurei imposicionem in capite ac tradicionem virge auree realiter investivimus Habendum et tenendum nomen stilum statum titulum honorem auctoritatem et dignitatem Ducis Norff prefato Duci et heredibus masculis de corpore suo exeuntibus imperpetuum Et ut idem Dux iuxta dicti nominis Ducis Norff decenciam et status sui nobilitatem possit honorificencius se gerere dedimus et concessimus et hac presenti carta nostra confirmavimus pro nobis et heredibus nostris prefato Duci Norff quadraginta libras habendas et annuatim percipiendas prefato Duci Norff et heredibus suis predictis imperpetuum de firmis exitibus proficuis et aliis comoditatibus quibuscumque de Com Norff et Suff provenientibus per manus vic eorundem Com pro tempore existentis ad terminos sancti Michaelis Archangeli et Pasche per equales porciones Eo quod expressa mencio de aliis donis sive concessionibus per nos eidem Duci ante hec tempora factis in presentibus facta non existit absque fine seu feodo pro presentibus huius nostre capiendo seu solvendo. Hiis testibus venerabilibus patribus Th. Cardinali Archiepiscopo Cantuar Th. London R. Bathon et Wellen et J. Lincoln Cancellario Anglie Episcopis Henrico Buk et Johanne Suff Ducibus Willelmo Arundell et Henrico Northumbr Comitibus Johanne Dudley de Dudley milite et Thoma Stanley de Stanley milite et aliis. Dat per manum nostram apud Westm vicesimo octavo die Junii.

per ipsum Regem et de dat etc

De creacione Comitis Notyngham

(7.)

R. Archiepiscopis etc salutem. Sciatis quod nos maiorum strenuitatem ac morum probitatem necnon scienciam fidelitatem et industriam quibus viget emicat atque pollet predilectus et fidelis consanguineus noster Willelmus Vicecomes Berkeley dominus de Berkeley ex nobili prosapia clarissimorum et illustrium virorum ducum Norff procreatus unius ex verorum et indubitatorum heredum Thome nuper et ultimi Ducis Norff intime ponderantes volentes que eundem Willelmum iuxta suorum exigentiam meritorum aliqualiter premiare de gracia nostra speciali ac ex certa sciencia et mero motu nostris ipsum consanguineum nostrum in Comitem Notyngham ereximus creavimus insignivimus prefecimus et ordinavimus ac nomen titulum statum stilum honorem auctoritatem et dignitatem Comitis Notyngham eidem consanguineo nostro damus et concedimus per presentes ac eum de nomine illo cum titulo statu stilo honore auctoritate et dignitate ceteris que honoribus eidem appendentibus et annexis per gladii cincturam realiter investivimus Habendum et tenendum nomen titulum statum stilum honorem auctoritatem et dignitatem Comitis Notyngham prefato consanguineo nostro et heredibus masculis de corpore suo exeuntibus imperpetuum Et ut idem Comes iuxta dicti nominis Comitis Notyngham decenciam et status sui nobilitatem possit hono

# Reign and Rebellion

## CONSPIRACY, DEFECTION, AND THE RISE OF HENRY TUDOR, JULY–NOVEMBER 1483

Once crowned, Richard III embarked on a dazzling royal progress that aimed to overcome lingering unease at the nature of his accession, and to promote his rightful claim to the throne in areas where he was well supported. Document 8, ***'Edward the bastard'***, shows how readily the new regime was accepted in some parts of the country.

From 29 August, Richard spent three weeks in York where he was received magnificently. The city truly celebrated the accession of their regional ruler, with few reservations about how he had attained the Crown. On 5 September Richard created his son Prince of Wales at York Minster. The King also perhaps announced his intention to establish a college of one hundred priests, and even to be buried in the church. He also reduced the civic taxes on the city. By such acts, Richard ensured that his royal favour continued to match the benevolence of his rule as Duke, and this was a central part of his very positive legacy in Yorkshire.

A terracotta bust of Henry VII, by Pietro Torrigiano. Torrigiano's work on this, and Henry VII's tomb, marked a new departure in English sculpture.

The bust was modelled towards the end of Henry's life, and suggests many of Henry's determined qualities. It also portrays a prematurely aged King, worn down by the fluctuations of dynastic politics: having achieved the throne, Henry VII spent over twenty years securing the Tudor Crown. The uncertain alliances that put him on the throne were undone by the appearance of Perkin Warbeck in 1491. Henry was not really free from Yorkist plotting until 1506. By then his wife and eldest son were also dead, and the Tudor dynasty remained precarious.

Once Richard had left London, however, his spies uncovered a plot to break into the Tower and free the Princes. No doubt expecting a backlash to his accession, Richard made certain he was fully aware of efforts to restore Edward V during the summer months. This was also the first time that Henry Tudor was mentioned in the context of rebellion against Richard.

Tudor's mother, Margaret Beaufort, at the heart of the conspiracy, may have hoped that a restored Edward V would allow her exiled

# 8 'Edward the bastard'

Particulars of the account of the alien subsidy of 1483 for Herefordshire (in Latin). In this document Edward V is described as 'Edward the bastard', perhaps suggesting some acceptance in the provinces of Richard's assertion that Edward V could not be king.

The collection of this tax on foreigners commenced under Edward IV but was halted at his death. Edward V's Council ordered new commissions on 27 April 1483. Only the counties of Herefordshire, Kent and London acted upon these instructions. These were perhaps the counties where the influence of the Woodville family was strongest. The Woodvilles controlled the new King, and by encouraging the county gentry to work quickly to their agenda in Edward V's name, there was a greater chance that they could force a continuity of authority.

In Herefordshire the commissions were headed by the Bishop of Worcester, president of the Prince's Council, and Sir Richard Croft, Edward's treasurer. However, once the Woodvilles were sidelined, Edward V deposed and Richard III was king, new commissions were issued. Richard promoted his friends and those previously overlooked, such as Lord Ferrers of Chartley and Sir John Lingen. Those collecting the tax soon adapted to the change of regime. In Herefordshire collectors had been appointed under Edward V, but the money they raised was not delivered to the Exchequer until 1484. By then, in this account, they refer to Edward V as 'Edward bastard late said King of England''.

This apparent reversal of attitude is striking. In April 1483 they were so keen to impress the new government of Edward V that only two other counties were able to match their speedy efficiency in starting the collection of the tax. By the following summer, their blunt dismissal of their former lord wholly reflected Richard III's own justifications in taking the throne. This indicates a clear awareness, even down the social scale, of the attitude that would best please the new Crown to ensure a continuance of service and influence.

This leather pouch was used to store Exchequer documents, including the one featured here. The text on it lists the contents of the documents within, for ease of reference.

**The first six lines of the text begin by stating that the document is the:**

Particulars of account of Edmund Brace of Pembridge, gentleman, John Lingen of Stoke by Leominster, gentleman, Robert Conningsby of Mancell, yeoman, Thomas Carpenter of Hereford, ironmonger, and Richard Woodward of Hereford, mercer [textile merchant], collectors of certain subsidies of aliens of the lord Edward King of England the fourth, granted by the commons of his realm of England in his parliament summoned and held at Westminster on the 20th of January in the 22nd year of his late [recent] reign, by the advice and assent of the lords spiritual and temporal in the same parliament then present to the honour of God and the realm of England, to be paid and levied in form following...

**The wording of the act is then recorded, with collection and payment targets. The particulars then go on to say that the details were enrolled on the eighth membrane of the memoranda roll of the Exchequer for Trinity Term of the first year of Richard III's reign.**

**Following the text of the parliamentary grant, the particulars continue eight lines from the bottom of the document with the following text:**

...that by letters of Edward the bastard, late said King of England under his great seal bearing date the 27 April in the first year of his reign, addressed to the reverend in God [John Alcock], by the same grace the Bishop of Worcester, and his trusty and well beloved James Baskerville, knight, Richard Croft, knight, Thomas Brugg, Thomas Braynton, Roger Bodnam and Henry Chamber, commissioners of the said Edward bastard late said king of England the fifth, in the said county of Hereford, by authority of these certain letters, the same commissioners have deputed and assigned the said Edmund Brace, John Lingen, Robert Conningsby, Thomas Carpenter and Richard Woodward to be collectors...

E

Com[itatus] Hereford

Dictus comp[otus] Edmundi Chace de Pembrugge Gentilman Joh[ann]is Lugwen de Stoke [illegible] Gentilman —
Gentilman Rob[er]ti Conyngesby de Aymestr[e] yoman Thome Carpenter de Hereford Iremonger
et Ric[ard]i Wodewarde de Hereford dyer collector[um] quor[un]dam subsid[iorum] alien[igenis] d[omi]no H[enrico] nunc Regi Angl[ie]
in [dicto com[itatu]] p[er] communitates regni sui Angl[ie] in parliamento suo apud Westm[onasterium] xx[mo] die Januarij anno xxxi[mo] dicti nunc
Regis summonito et tento de assensu dominorum spiritualium et temporalium in eodem parliamento tunc
existencium ad honorem dei et regni Regis Angl[ie] [illegible] concess[orum] soluend[orum] et leuand[orum] modo et forma sub
sequente videlicet de qualibet persona extranea infra regnum Angl[ie] non nata nec indigena hospicium infra idem
regnum tenente vj s. viij d. [illegible] infra terras Hibernie et Wall[ie] ac in villa nostra [illegible] et
ponte eiusdem necnon in villa Cales' et Marchie eiusdem ac in omnibus insulis sub obediencia dicti nunc Regis
[illegible] similiter natis existent sub obediencia sua except[is] et religiosis et si duo vel tres vel plures [illegible]
vel plures in unius [illegible] manentes in uno hospicio vel domum tenuerint [illegible] quilibet eorum soluat eidem subsidio
vj s. viij d. Et de eodem de qualibet persona non indigena nec infra regnum predictum [illegible] insulis [villis] limites et inde nata
nec sub obediencia dicti nunc Regis nata infra regnum suum existente hospicium non tenente vel commorantibus
husbondes omnibus religiosis et de qualibet persona non indigena except[is] [illegible]
[illegible] et tenent xx d. necnon de quolibet mercatore [illegible] [illegible] [illegible] [illegible] [illegible]
[illegible] [illegible] et [illegible] et de [illegible] [illegible] [illegible] [illegible] et [illegible] infra [illegible]
et quolibet alio [illegible] [illegible] dictum regnum suum Angl[ie] [illegible] [illegible] hospicium tenente [illegible]
commorante infra [illegible] regnum suum Angl[ie] [illegible] [illegible] [illegible] [illegible] [illegible] et [illegible] communi
religiosis [illegible] de quolibet [illegible] [illegible] [illegible] [illegible] [illegible] [illegible] [illegible] et [illegible] [illegible]
[illegible] vel [illegible] de [illegible] [illegible] [illegible] et de quolibet alio [illegible] [illegible] [illegible] [illegible] [illegible] [illegible]
[illegible] et [illegible] dicti nunc Regis [illegible] nato non indigena [illegible] et [illegible] infra dictum regnum suum Angl[ie]
infra dictum regnum suum hospicium minime tenente vel in aliquo loco sub obediencia dicti nunc Regis [illegible]
[illegible] [illegible] [illegible] vel [illegible] [illegible] aliquo commorante xx d. [illegible] [illegible] [illegible]
dicti nunc Regis [illegible] [illegible] [illegible] [illegible] [illegible] [illegible] [illegible] soluend[um] et leuand[um] prout in eodem
[illegible] [illegible] [illegible] [illegible] [illegible] in memorand[is] [illegible] de anno [illegible] Regis nunc [illegible]
[illegible] videlicet [illegible] [illegible] [illegible] [illegible] [illegible] anno primo [illegible] [illegible] [illegible]
Regis [illegible] H[enrici] [illegible] nunc dicti Regis Angl[ie] quinti de magno sigillo suo [illegible] xxvj[mo] die Aprilis
anno regni sui primo [illegible] [illegible] [illegible] [illegible] [illegible] [illegible] [illegible] [illegible] [illegible]
et fidelibus suis Jacobo [illegible] militi [illegible] [illegible] militi Thome [illegible] Thome [illegible] [illegible]
[illegible] et Henrico [illegible] Commissionar[iis] dicti H[enrici] [illegible] nunc dicti R[egis] Angl[ie] quinti in dicto
Com[itatu] Hereford [illegible] [illegible] [illegible] [illegible] Commissionar[ii] [illegible] et assignaverunt predictos Edmundum Chace
Johannem Lugwen Robertum Conyngesby Thomam Carpenter et Ricardum Wodewarde collectores [illegible]
[illegible] [illegible] continetur in [illegible] [illegible] [illegible] videlicet de [illegible] [illegible] [illegible] [illegible] [illegible] —
[illegible] [illegible] [illegible] [illegible] [illegible] [illegible]

son to recover his estates as Earl of Richmond. Alternatively, Margaret and Elizabeth Woodville may have been sure that Edward V was dead, and therefore acted to maintain the momentum of opposition to Richard before his rule became established. The involvement of the two matriarchs ensured that Tudor's position as a claimant advanced rapidly at this time. His promise at Christmas 1483 to marry Elizabeth of York signified an acceptance of his status as a rival to Richard III.

Micklegate Bar. This was the gate of York through which Richard arrived in the summer of 1483. It was also where his father's head had been displayed after the Battle of Wakefield in 1460. Even after Bosworth, some support for the dead King continued within the city, despite Henry VII's forceful policy toward the Ricardian north. A group of city goldsmiths, led by Thomas Wrangwashe, allowed rebels to enter the city in 1489, and as late as 1491 a discussion of Richard's reputation, in which he was allegedly described as a hypocrite and a crookback, sparked a brawl.

By mid-September Richard had ordered weapons in expectation of further risings. It is likely that if the Princes were not already dead, they would have met their end at this time, as conspiracies in their name became better organized and more threatening.

At some point during September, the Duke of Buckingham also rebelled. The Bishop of Ely, then in the Duke's custody, has been credited with persuading Buckingham that the preservation of his power depended on opposing Richard. The Duke may also have been concerned at his own prospects if a nonentity like Henry Tudor did become king.

At the beginning of October, Richard was fully aware of Buckingham's plans, but was prepared to wait for the rebels to declare themselves (see document 9, ***Securing control***). Buckingham may have hoped or planned that the Stanley family would also throw their weight against Richard once the rebellion started. Lord Stanley's heir, George, Lord Strange, did lead a large army from Lancashire during October, but declined to commit it to either side during the uprising. The neutrality of the Stanleys gave Richard a clear advantage.

By 10 October risings had occurred in Kent and quickly spread westwards along the southern counties. The men involved were old household servants of Edward IV, such as Sir John Guildford in Kent, and Sir Giles Daubeney in Somerset. The uprisings were serious but uncoordinated, and John Howard, Duke of Norfolk, was able to secure London and pressurize rebels in Kent and Essex.

The King headed to Salisbury from Nottingham, and acted decisively to block Buckingham's advance. A combination of poor weather and a total lack of support in the Welsh Marches left Buckingham isolated. He was eventually betrayed by a servant and captured in Shropshire. Brought to Richard at Salisbury, he was refused an audience and beheaded on 2 November.

Queen Elizabeth Woodville. The Queen is depicted here as a sister of the Fraternity of the Blessed Virgin. In reality, Elizabeth was manipulative and arrogant, and used her power over King Edward to secure her own position and to advance the dominance of the Woodville faction at court.

# 9 *Securing control*

Richard's letter (in English) to the Lord Chancellor (John Russell, Bishop of Lincoln), dated 12 October 1483, requesting that the Great Seal be brought to him in Lincoln.

Richard's anger at Buckingham's treason is almost palpable in this famous letter. Since there had been previous correspondence, it has been assumed that Richard knew Buckingham was actively involved in the rebellion at least by 10 October, if not earlier. The fury that Richard unleashes here against his former ally and confidant – 'the most untrue creature living' – suggests that the news of Buckingham's defection was a bitter blow to the King, and Richard's merciless treatment of the Duke after his capture certainly bears this out.

The section written in the King's hand is a personal intervention seldom seen on such warrants, and implies great urgency on the King's part to get control of the machinery of government in his own hands as quickly as possible. The Great Seal authenticated documents with the highest authority, and Richard may not have been wholly confident that Russell would be able to get to Lincoln if he delayed any longer – it seems Russell had already made excuses that his ill health, 'certain infirmities and diseases', prevented him from journeying sooner. This could be why Richard asked for trusted Chancery officers to come with the Seal and news immediately upon the sight of the letter: evidently Richard knew of Buckingham's plans and may have been concerned that he would head for the capital in an attempt to take control of government. By relocating the means of exercising government, Richard was taking a wise precaution, perhaps based on his knowledge of risings against Edward IV.

## RICHARD'S LETTER READS:

Right reverend father in God, right trusty and wellbeloved we greet you well. And in our heartiest wise [manner] thank you for the manifold [numerous] presents that your servants on your behalf have presented unto us at that our being here, which we assure you we took and accepted with good heart, and so we have cause. And whereas we by God's grace intend briefly to advance us towards our rebel and traitor the duke of Buckingham to resist and withstand his malicious purpose as lately by our letters we certified [informed] you (of) our mind more at large [at length]. For which cause it behoves [is appropriate for] us to have our great seal here. We being informed that for certain infirmities and diseases as you sustain you may not in your person to your ease conveniently come unto us with the same. Wherefore we desire and nevertheless charge you that forthwith upon the sight of these [letters] you safely do the same our great seal to be sent unto us, and such of the officers of our Chancery as by your wisdom shall be thought necessary. Receiving these our letters for your sufficient discharge [authority to act] in that behalf. Given under our signet at our city of Lincoln, the 12th day of October

### In Richard's own hand:

We would most gladly you came yourself if that you may, and if you may not we pray you not to fail but to accomplish in all diligence our said commandment to send our seal incontinent [immediately] upon the sight hereof as we trust you with such as we trust, and the officers pertaining to attend with it, praying you to ascertain us of your news. Here, loved be God, is all well and truly determined and for to resist the duke of Buckingham the most untrue creature living, whom with God's grace we shall not be long until that we will be in that [*sic*, those] parts and subdue his malice. We assure you that never was false traitor better provided for [treated] as this bearer, Gloucester, can show.

By the kyng

Right reverend fader in god right trusty and welbeloved we grete you wele And in oure hertiest wyse
thanke you for the manyfold presentes that youre servantes on youre behalve have presented unto us at this oure
beyng here whiche we assure you we toke and accepted with good hert and so we have cause And whereas
we by goddes grace entende briefly to avaunce us towardes oure rebell and traytoure the Duc of
Bukyngham to resiste and withstande his malicious purpose as lately by oure other lettres we certified
you oure mynde more at large ffor whiche cause it behoveth us to have oure grete seale here we beyng
enfourmed that for suche infirmitees and diseases as ye sustene ye may not in youre persone to youre ease
conveniently come unto us with the same Wherfor we desire and natheles charge you that forthwith
upon the sight of thees ye saufly doo the same oure grete seale to be sent unto us and suche of thoffice
of oure Chauncerie as by youre wisedom shalbe thought necessarie receyvyng thees oure lettres for youre
sufficient discharge in that behalve Yeven under oure signet at oure Citie of Lincoln the xij day
of October

We wolde most gladly ye came youre selff yf that
ye may and yf ye may not we pray you not to fayle but
to acomplyshe in all dyllygence our sayde commaundement to
sende our seale incontinent apon the syght heroff as we truste
you with such as ye truste and the offycers pertaynyng to attend with hyt
prayng you to ascertayne us of your newes ther. Here loved be god ys
all well and trewly determyned and for to resyste the malysse
of hym that hadde best cawse to be trewe th' Duc of Bokyngham
the most untrewe creature lyvyng whom with Gods grace we shall not
be long tyll that we wyll be in that partyes and subdewe hys malys.
We assure you ther was never falsse traytor better purveyde for as this berrer Gloucestre shall schew you.

The King's forces then moved towards Exeter, arriving around 8 November, and dispersed the rebels as they went. Henry Tudor's involvement was restricted to a feeble attempted landing around this time, but the coast was guarded and he was forced to withdraw across the channel to Brittany.

Many of the rebels of 1483 were from key southern families, connected by marriage and their experienced service to Edward IV. These were just the men Richard had hoped to win over to his regime. Although the north and midlands remained loyal, a large group of southerners had found Richard's kingship unacceptable. Rather than submit to his authority, they rebelled and joined Henry Tudor in exile abroad. This development made it vital that Richard established effective lordship in the south before his enemies regrouped and launched another invasion.

Many of Richard's northern retainers, already in the south as part of his army, took over posts as sheriffs and constables of castles. They confiscated rebels' lands, and headed commissions to prosecute those captured. New appointees were drawn from elsewhere, and Richard also pardoned some others who would submit, but the overall impression was of a plantation of northerners into the south.

In England more generally, most of the experienced peerage and senior clergy did nothing to jeopardize their status as long as Richard was in control. In families like the Howards, de la Poles and Herberts, Richard did have firm allies who took on extended responsibilities within the regime. Even men like Thomas, Lord Stanley – who was doing well out of Richard's patronage despite a history of animosity – had much to lose by being anything but expedient until Richard was either victorious or vanquished.

This portrait of Margaret Beaufort remains in St John's College, Cambridge, the foundation of which she began just before her death in 1509. The image reflects Margaret's genuine piety, but she was also a skilled politician and expert conspirator. That Henry Tudor even became a challenger to Richard III's Crown was largely due to Margaret's forceful involvement in the politics of the 1480s.

A Parliament was originally called for 2 November, but Buckingham's rebellion disrupted preparations. It finally met on 23 January, and although we have no evidence of the knights that attended in the Commons, the appointment of William Catesby as Speaker suggests that only representatives sympathetic to the new King were elected. The main acts established Richard's title (see document 10, ***Richard's claim to the throne***) and attainted the rebels of the previous year, including Henry Tudor.

During the session, Richard required the lords, bishops and members of the royal household to swear an oath of loyalty to Edward, Prince of Wales, should Richard be deposed or killed. Soon after Parliament ended, the King again showed evidence of his true title to the leaders of the London livery companies. Through these meetings, Richard was preparing a foundation for the dynastic and financial future of his heir.

## RICHARD'S KINGSHIP, 1483–5

The remainder of Richard's reign, in an administrative, financial and legal sense, offers few indications of how he might have shaped the monarchy and mechanisms of royal government. The establishment of the Council of the North continued his benevolent noble lordship, and also suggests that Richard did have a genuine motivation to maintain impartial justice. The royal Council, too, was encouraged to favour petitions from poor and deprived subjects.

There is certainly evidence of a frequent reassertion from Richard of his belief in the forcefulness of the coronation oath to uphold the law and defend justice. This can be seen in surviving proclamations, in instructions to officers of royal estates, and in records of less formal gatherings of judges and councillors. The chance survival of Richard's book of signet letters demonstrates his personal involvement in government more closely than for Edward IV, but it does not reveal any great innovation during his short reign.

Richard also changed the personnel of the regime where necessary, but he was obliged to maintain the structures of government operated by Edward IV. Richard continued to divert the management of royal finance to the chamber of the household, and not the Exchequer, and he also extended the use of recognizances (legal bonds or obligations, for example see document 14) to control political suspects – both frequently seen as Tudor developments.

Royal revenues were drained by the costs of defeating the 1483 rebellion, in campaigning against the Scots in 1484, and in preparing for Tudor's expected landing. Richard assented to a popular act in the Parliament of 1484 outlawing the forced gifts or benevolences that his brother had demanded. Unusually, he did not ask Parliament for any grant of taxation, despite war with the Scots, and he refused cash gifts from towns visited on his first progress as King.

This could suggest an intention to live solely on royal revenues, which would have appealed to both MPs and subjects. He did have his northern estates and the forfeitures from 1483 to draw upon. Instructions to officials in 1484 requiring a tightening of procedures suggest a wish to maximize income quickly and efficiently. However, this has been accepted as evidence of a growing financial crisis and not of the King's hope to avoid burdening taxpayers.

In 1485 Richard was forced to approach his leading supporters for loans. It seemed that only the destruction of Tudor would enable royal finances to be stabilized, and allow Richard to develop his own style of kingship.

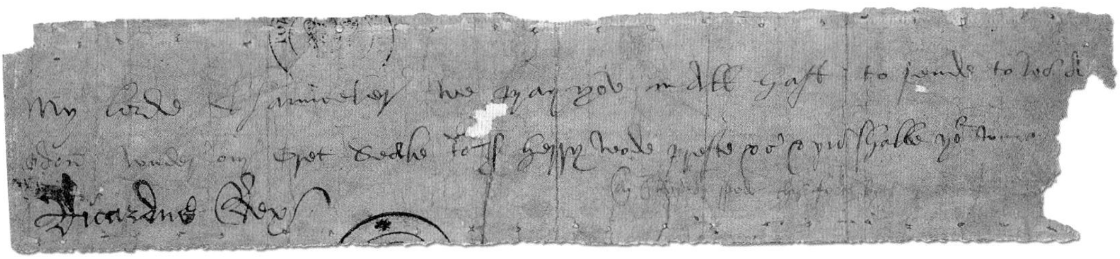

Detail from a warrant for the Great Seal, showing an example of Richard's signature. Such warrants were the final instructions to the Lord Chancellor to create letters patent; this particular one, dated 1484, is requesting a letter of pardon for Henry Wood, priest.

# 10 *Richard's claim to the throne*

Two extracts from the *Titulus Regius* ('Royal Title'), Richard's official justification for taking the throne, as presented to Parliament in 1484. It is one of the most important and unusual documents from Richard III's reign. Although it is a formal record of Parliament, it claims to be the text of a petition passed to the King by a selection of Lords and Commons in June 1483, begging him to take the throne for the well-being of the realm. To quell any fears that this was not a genuine expression of will, the text of the petition was presented to Richard's first Parliament in January 1484.

Written in English, the *Titulus Regius* sets out definitively Richard's claim to the throne. It is not difficult to see why it has been dismissed as blatant propaganda. The Act casts Edward IV's reign as the centre of all moral corruption and feckless government (which it certainly was not), and lists the effects of Edward's sordid marriage to a most unsuitable widow, who used witchcraft to ensnare him. It claims that, through his preoccupation with lust, Edward has managed to undo the perfectly balanced and prosperous rule of his royal predecessors. Furthermore, the scandal of his adulterous marriage makes it impossible for his children to inherit the Crown. The claim of Richard's other nephew Edward, Earl of Warwick, is by-passed with the citation of his (reversible) attainder. By contrast, Richard's own skills and virtues are championed. The emphasis is on Richard's embodiment of the rightful claim of his father Richard, Duke of York, and contrasts this with an oblique reference to Edward IV's illegitimacy.

The document concludes with an invocation of Parliament to endorse Richard's right, title and estate as king. It is important as an example of how the authority of late medieval parliaments could be manipulated to express the king's personal agenda.

## THE *TITULUS REGIUS*:

...And how also, that at the time of contract of the same pretended marriage, and before and long time after, the said King Edward was and stood [as good as] married and troth plight [pledged] to one Dame Eleanor Butler, daughter of the old Earl of Shrewsbury, with whom the same King Edward had made a precontract of matrimony, long time before he made the said pretended marriage with the said Elizabeth Grey [Elizabeth Woodville], in manner and form abovesaid. Which premises being true, as in very truth they been [be] true, it appears and follows evidently, that the said King Edward during his life, and the said Elizabeth, lived together sinfully and damnably in adultery, against the law of God and of his Church; and therefore no marvel that the Sovereign Lord and the Head of this land, being of such ungodly disposition, and provoking the ire and indignation of our Lord God, such heinous mischiefs and inconveniences, as is above remembered, were used and committed in the realm among the subjects. Also it appears evidently and follows, that all the issue and children of the said King Edward, being bastards, and unable to inherit or to claim any thing by inheritance, by the law and custom of England...

...Over this we consider, how that you be the undoubted son and heir of Richard, late Duke of York, very inheritor to the said Crown and Dignity Royal [status of kingship], and as in right King of England, by way of inheritance; and that at this time, the premises duly considered, there is no one other person living but you only, that by right may claim the said Crown and Dignity Royal, by way of inheritance, and how that you be born within this land; by reason wherof, as we deem in our minds, you be more naturally inclined to the prosperity and common weal [commonwealth] of the same; and all the three estates of the land have, and may have, more certain knowledge of your birth and affiliation abovesaid. We consider also, the great wit, prudence, justice, princely courage, and the memorable and laudable acts in diverse battles, which as we by experience know you heretofore have done, for the salvation and defence of this same realm; and also the great noblesse [nobility] and excellence of your birth and blood, as of him that is descended of the three most royal houses in Christendom, that is to say, England, France, and Spain ...

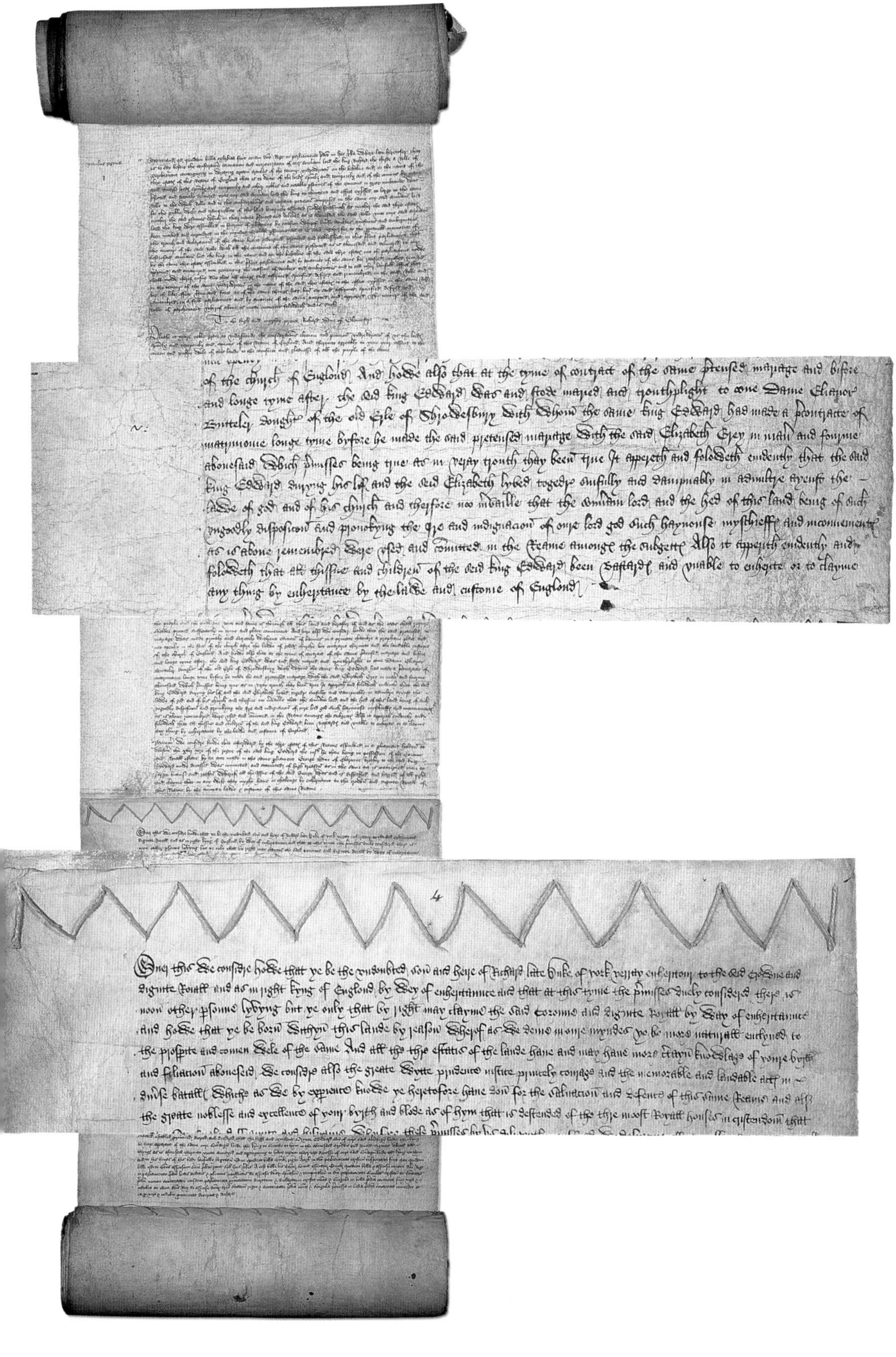
of the chirch of Englond And howe also that at the tyme of contract of the same pretensed mariage and bifore
and longe tyme after the seid king Edward was and stode maried and trouthplight to oone Dame Elianor
Butteler doughter of the old Erle of Shrewesbury with whom the same king Edward had made a precontracte of
matrimonie longe tyme bifore he made the said pretensed mariage with the said Elizabeth Grey in maner and fourme
abovesaid Which premisses being true as in veray trouth thay been true it appereth and foloweth evidently that the said
king Edward duryng his lif and the seid Elizabeth lyved togedr synfully and dampnably in adultre ayenst the
lawe of god and of his chirch and therfore noo mervaille that the souverain lord and the hed of this land being of such
ungodly disposicion and provokyng the ire and indignacion of oure lord god such haynouse myschieffs and inconvenients
as is above remembred were used and commytted in the Reame amonge the subgettes Also it appereth evidently and
foloweth that all thissue and children of the seid king Edward been bastards and unable to enherite or to clayme
any thing by enheritance by the lawe and custome of Englond
4
Over this we considre howe that ye be the undoubted son and heire of Richard late Duke of York verray enheritour to the seid Corone and
dignite Roiall and as in right kyng of Englond by wey of enheritaunce and that at this tyme the premisses duely considered ther is
noon other persone lyvyng but ye only that by right may clayme the said Corone and dignite royall by wey of enheritaunce
And howe that ye be born withyn this lande by reason wherof as we deme in oure myndes ye be more naturall enclyned to
the prosperite and comen wele of the same And all the thre estates of the lande have and may have more certayn knowlage of youre byrth
and filiation aboveseid We considre also the greate witte prudence justice princely corage and the memorable and laudable acts in
diverse batalls whiche as we by experience knowe ye heretofore have don for the salvacion and defence of this same Reame And also
the greate noblesse and excellence of your byrth and blode as of hym that is descended of the thre moost Royall houses in cristendom that

227
242
Baron
Cornwall
Melton
Britton
to borow
Esperance me
comfort

# Bosworth and Richard's Legacy under Henry VII

## RICHARD'S TUDOR RIVAL

The King and Queen were again on progress north in April 1484, preparing for the military campaign against Scotland, when they received the devastating news of the death of Edward, Prince of Wales. The royal couple spent a month in deep reflection at Nottingham Castle and the Scottish invasion was scaled down. The crushing blow dealt by Edward's death forced the King to focus all his efforts on eliminating the Tudor threat to his now precarious dynasty.

A later impression, probably from the seventeenth century, of what Richard's banner at Bosworth may have looked like. This page also contains heraldic images from the arms of some other late fifteenth-century gentry families.

Both Edward IV and Richard had attempted to prise Tudor and his supporters from Brittany, where he had been exiled since 1471. Fluctuations in influence between pro- and anti-French factions within the Breton court made it difficult for the English to follow a consistent policy. In France too, Louis, Duke of Orléans sought to involve Brittany in his power struggle with Charles VIII's Regent, Anne of Beaujeu.

Richard offered archers to help defend the Breton border in summer 1484, and almost forced an agreement to have Tudor arrested. Henry's supporters were alerted at the last minute and he was able to escape into France. By October, Tudor was at the court of King Charles, where he provided a convenient foreign policy opportunity for the pressurized French regime.

With French backing, Henry was presented, improbably, as a son of Henry VI and a Lancastrian claimant. He circulated a letter in England asking for support, and claimed the throne directly in his own right. Richard's response was the vitriolic proclamation of December 1484 (see document 11, ***Tudor the traitor***).

Richard's agents were probably aware at the end of April 1485 that French preparations were underway for Tudor's invasion. At the beginning of May, the King left Westminster. He spent some time with his mother at Berkhamsted before reaching Nottingham by 9 June, where he awaited news of Tudor's landing.

At the same time, peace negotiations between France and Brittany suddenly ended Tudor's usefulness as a bargaining tool, and his cause was officially dropped. Tudor had acquired professional troops recently discharged from campaigns in Flanders, but they were to be paid through loans. The only Yorkist nobles in Henry's entourage, Thomas, Marquis of Dorset and John Bourchier, Lord FitzWarin, were to be left in Paris as security.

Tudor's small force that sailed in 1485 was scraped together from personal pledges and loans. With little chance of sympathetic risings in England, his cause looked bleaker than in 1483. He landed at Milford Haven on 7 August. Richard received this news on 11 August when he began to summon his leading supporters to Nottingham. While Tudor marched cautiously through Wales, King Richard and nobles such as Northumberland and Norfolk had mustered their followers at Leicester by 18 August. Having waited for so long for his enemy to emerge, Richard had to act swiftly to undermine the rival king's position, and to confront him in battle.

A modern replica of Richard's banner on Ambion Hill, the traditional site of the Battle of Bosworth. Surviving evidence for the course of the battle and those present is either very sketchy or produced from less than trustworthy sources, such as the Stanley sponsored poems *The Ballad of Bosworth Field* and *The Song of Lady Bessy* (Elizabeth of York). Recent work now suggests that Richard's defeat was a very narrow one caused by innovative tactics from Tudor's mercenaries and the intervention of Sir William Stanley at a moment when Richard's victory looked likely.

At a meeting near Atherstone on 21 August, Tudor attempted to persuade Lord Stanley to join him. Stanley forces had been shadowing the invader's advance through Shropshire, but Stanley's heir, Lord Strange, was with Richard as security for his father's loyal behaviour. Once again, neither Lord Stanley, nor his brother Sir William, would commit their separate forces to either side.

Tudor's army of mercenaries and assorted small companies camped near Merevale Abbey on the night of 21 August. Richard left Leicester the same day with a large force comprised of the soldiers of the nobles who had backed his seizure of the throne. He had every reason to be confident.

## 22 AUGUST 1485: THE FOCAL POINT OF RICHARD'S LIFE

The Battle of Bosworth has been re-sited a number of times. The names of the leading figures actually present, and the exact details of the course of the fighting are still hidden by a lack of detailed evidence. However, some very recent work has suggested another alternative battlefield, at a site closer to Merevale

# 11 *Tudor the traitor*

The proclamation against Henry Tudor, December 1484: this is the official two-page draft (in English) sent to the Lord Chancellor for him to copy, under Richard's seal, and distribute. The document was composed by Richard and his close councillors and would have been proclaimed at markets and fairs by officers of the county sheriffs.

The proclamation draws out many of the contradictions associated with the modern view of Richard III's character. Firstly, there is unfounded propaganda in reports that Henry Tudor had sold the English claim to France in return for French help. A further assertion that Tudor's invading force planned to murder and pillage their way through the countryside once they landed, suggests that his supporters were a rabble of exiles and mercenaries, led, but not controlled by, an unproved and unknown outsider. Tudor was a traitor, and his supporters had abandoned their country and placed themselves under the protection of England's enemies. If they were willing to do this, then maybe any scandalous agreement with the French was possible. This kind of propaganda was perhaps crude, but it was vital in contrasting Richard as an anointed and experienced king with a would-be usurper who was also an illegitimate foreigner.

Richard's good lordship and inspiring leadership is declared forcefully. He urges Englishmen to defend their families and inheritances. The King himself will lead by example: as a well-willed and diligent prince he will put himself to the same labour and effort as that expected from his own loyal supporters. Richard also merges his own position as king with the well-being of the realm. This cleverly suggests that good national rule depends upon his continued personal kingship.

The text shows Richard as fully confident of the weakness of Henry Tudor's claims to the throne through lineal descent, and of his own right to rule and the support he expected. The message projected here is of a king prepared and ready to resist his challenger, and to fully and clearly establish his right to rule. We cannot truly know if this was a display of genuine confidence, or a device to bolster flagging support.

## THE PROCLAMATION READS:

By the King

Proclamation Right reverend father in God right trusty and well beloved we greet you well. And will and charge you that under our great seal being in your keeping you do make out as many proclamations after the form following as you shall think expedient to be delivered to the sheriffs of our counties (of) within this our realm. For as much as the king our sovereign lord has certain knowledge that Piers Bishop of Exeter, Thomas Grey late [recently] Marquis of Dorset, Jasper late Earl of Pembroke, John late Earl of Oxford and Sir Edward Woodville with other divers his rebels and traitors disabled and attainted by authority of the high court of parliament, of whom many being known for open murderers, adulterers and extortioners contrary to truth, honour and nature have forsaken their natural country, taking them first to be under the obedience of the Duke of Brittany and to him promised certain things which by him and his council were thought things too greatly unnatural and abominable for them to grant, observe, keep and perform. And therefore the same utterly refused, they seeing that the said Duke and his council would not aid and succour them nor follow their ways, privily [secretly] departed out of his country into France, there taking them to be under the obedience of the King's ancient enemy Charles calling himself King of France. And to abuse and blind the commons of this said realm the said rebels and traitors have chosen to be their captain (one) Henry, late calling himself Earl of Richmond which of his ambitious and insatiable covetousness stirred and excited by the confederacy of the King's said rebels and traitors encroaches upon him the name and title of royal estate of this realm of England. Whereunto he has no manner, interest, right or colour [quality] as every man well knows. And to the intent to achieve the same by the aid, support and assistance of the King's said ancient enemies and of this his realm has covenanted and bargained with him and with all the council of France to give up and release in perpetuity all the title and claim that kings of England have had and ought to have to the crown and realm of France. Together with all the duchies of Normandy, Gascony and Guyenne, castles and towns of Calais, Guisnes, [and] Hammes with the marches pertaining to the same. And over this and beside the alienation of all the premises into the possession of the King's said ancient enemies to the greatest dishonour shame and rebuke that ever might fall to this land, the said Henry, Earl of Richmond and all the other the King's rebels and traitors aforesaid have intended at their coming to do the most cruel

**Second page**

murders, slaughters, robberies and disinheritances that ever were seen in any Christian realm. … And our said sovereign lord as a well willed, diligent and courageous prince will put his most royal person to all labour and pain necessary in this behalf for the resistance and subduing of his said enemies, rebels, and traitors to the most comfort, well and surety of all and singular his true and faithful liegemen and subjects. And these our letters shall be therein your warrant given under our signet at our palace of Westminster the 7th day of December the second year of our reign

To the right reverend father in God our right trusty and well-beloved the Bishop of Lincoln our Chancellor of England

R

By the king

Proclamacio Right Reverend fader in god right trusty and welbeloved We grete you wele
And woll and charge you that undre oure grete seale being in your keping
ye doo make out asmany proclamacions after the fourme folowing as ye shal
think expedient to be directed to the Shireffs of alle the counties within
V this oure Royaume / fforsomoche as the king oure soverain lorde hath certaine
knowlege that Piers Bisshop of Exeter Thomas Grey late Marques
dorset Jasper late Erle of Pembroke John late Erle of Oxenford and Sir
Edward Wodevile with other diverse his Rebelles and traitours disabled and
atteynted by auctorite of the high Courte of parlement of whom many be
knowen for open murdrers advoutrers and extorcioners contrary to trouthe
honoure and nature have forsaken theire naturall contre taking them first
to be undre thobeissaunce of the duc of Bretaigne and to him promysed
certain thinges whiche by him and his counsell were thought thinges to
gretely unnaturall and abhomynable for them to graunt observe kepe and
performe And therfor the same utterly refused They seing that the said
Duc and his counsell wolde not ayde and socoure them ner folowe theire
wayes prively departed out of his countrey into ffraunce there taking
them to be undre thobeissaunce of the kinges auncient enemy Charles
calling himself king of ffraunce and to abuse and blynde the comons of
this said Royaume the said Rebelles and traitours have chosen to be theire
Capitain oon Henry late calling himself Erle of Richemond whiche
of his ambicious and insaciable covetise stirred and excited by the confederacie
of the kinges said Rebelles and traitours encrocheth upon him the name and
title of Royall estate of this Royaume of England whereunto he hath no maner
interesse right or colour as every man wele knoweth And to thentent
to acheve the same by thaide support and assistence of the kinges said
auncient enemyes and of this his Royaume hath covenaunted and bargayned
with them and with all the counsell of ffraunce to yeve up and relesse
in perpetuite all the title and clayme that kinges of England have had
and ought to have to the Corone and Royaume of ffraunce togider with
the duchies of Normandie Gascoigne and Guyen Castelles and townes
of Caleis Guysnes Hammes with the marches pertenyng to the same
And over this and beside the alienacion of all the premisses into the
possession of the kinges said auncient enemyes to the grettest anyentisment
shame and rebuke that ever might falle to this lande the said Henry
Erle of Richemond and all the other the kinges Rebelles and traitours
aforesaid have extended at theire comyng to doo the most cruell

Thomas Lord Stanley, 1st Earl of Derby's garter plate from St George's Chapel, Windsor. Stanley's careful progress through the extreme political upheavals from the 1450s onwards is the finest example of how late fifteenth-century noblemen could survive and prosper by avoiding enthusiastic participation in events. By advancing his family's interests ruthlessly, Stanley benefited from the fall of more partisan contemporaries – including his own brother, Sir William, in 1495.

and Atherstone, six miles from the traditional vicinity of Ambion Hill and Dadlington (Henry VII compensated local landowners after the battle; see document 12 *'Our late victorious field'*). New French evidence has also provided a clearer picture of Tudor's unexpected victory.

Many sources emphasize Richard's troubled dreams and poor planning before the battle. It is likely that on 22 August 1485 he would have been apprehensive but exhilarated – this moment was the culmination of years of preparation. With Richard finally able to face Tudor in person, victory would enable him to put his troubled first years behind him, and give God's blessing to a long and prosperous reign.

Late medieval infantry weapons. For much of the medieval period the weapons of footsoldiers resembled agricultural implements or hunting weapons. Infantrymen armed with long-shafted weapons such as polearms, glaives, Moorish pikes, halbards and hooked bills formed the massed ranks. From the mid-fifteenth century, the Swiss in particular began to drill and train massed units of pikemen to fight as a coherent group.

The wars between Burgundy and France of the 1470s then saw the first use of expert pike formations at battles such as Grandson in 1476. The blade in the centre of this image most closely resembles that of a late medieval pike (although it would normally be smaller and more pointed). Pikes were usually 14–20 feet long, and were used in staggered ranks to push back enemy units. Archers, hand gunners or billmen would then exploit any gaps that appeared in the opposing line. It now appears that just such a formation withstood and broke Richard's cavalry charge at Bosworth.

# 12 'Our late victorious field'

Compensation paid by Henry VII to the Abbot of Merevale (Miravale) for damage to his land, and to townships suffering loss of crops, as a result of the Battle of Bosworth, November and December 1485.

These two documents (in English) provide evidence that the Battle of Bosworth was fought nearer to Atherstone than the current site north of the village of Dadlington. In the first warrant, Henry VII offers a payment of £72 2s 4d to townships that had suffered damage to their harvest crops by the armies 'at our late victorious field'. This seems to refer to the battle site itself, rather than to the location of musters or movements before the fighting commenced. The battle may well have destroyed the harvest within these parishes, and John Fox and John Atherston could have been the representatives selected to petition the Crown for some form of compensation to cover the loss of their valuable crop.

In the second warrant Henry VII offers compensation to the Abbot of Merevale for losses and damage caused by his army passing through the abbey when 'coming toward our late field', *i.e.* when marching towards the battle site. The third continuation of the *Crowland Chronicle* states that Henry encamped near the Abbey on the night before the battle, so the warrant for compensation may be consistent with the damage caused by the camp of several thousand soldiers. This would place Tudor's forces in the vicinity of the abbey on the morning of the battle. The same chronicle goes on to state that the battle itself was fought near Merevale.

The restriction of payments to Merevale Abbey and the surrounding parishes does suggest that the fighting was contained within an area marked by the townships of Atherstone, Mancetter, Ratcliffe Culey, and Atterton. Other places must have suffered similar losses and damage as the armies manoeuvred and assembled before 22 August, but Henry VII's payments here may represent a specific charitable gift to the parishes directly associated with his unexpected victory.

## THE FIRST WARRANT READS:

Henry by the grace of God King of England and of France and Lord of Ireland, to the Treasurer and Chamberlains of our Exchequer, greeting. We will and charge you that unto our wellbeloved subjects Sir John Fox, parson of Witherley, and John Atherston, gentleman, you pay and deliver in ready money immediately upon the sight hereof the sum of three score (and) twelve pounds, two shillings and four pence sterling which we of our charity have appointed [fixed by agreement] them to have. And to deliver the same to certain townships which sustained losses of their corns and grains by us and our company at our late victorious field for their due recompense in that behalf. That is to say, Atherstone, £20; Witherley, £13; Atterton, £8 10s; Fenny Drayton £20; Mancetter £5 19s; Atherstone £4 13s 4d. Not setting any impress [loan] or other charge upon them or any of them for for the same. Any act, ordinance [arrangement], or restraint to the contrary not withstanding. And these our letters shall be your sufficient warrant in that part. Given under our privy seal at our palace of Westminster the 29th day of November, the first year of our reign.

## THE SECOND WARRANT READS:

Henry by the grace of God King of England and of France and Lord of Ireland, to the Treasurer and Chamberlains of our Exchequer, greeting. Where as verily we understand that our right wellbeloved in God, the Abbot of our monastery of Miravale had and sustained great hurts, charges and losses by the occasion of the great repair and resort that our people coming toward our late field made, as well unto the house of Miravale aforesaid, as in going over his ground to the destruction of his corns and pastures. We let you know that we, in recompense of the same, have given and granted unto him the sum of 100 marks sterling to be had and perceived [received] of our reward. Wherefore, we will and charge you that you unto the said Abbot make contentation and payment of the said sum of 100 marks in ready money without imprest [loan] or other charge to be set upon him for the same. And these our letters shall be your sufficient warrant and discharge against us in that behalf. Given under our privy seal at our palace of Westminster,
the 7th day of December, the first year of our reign.

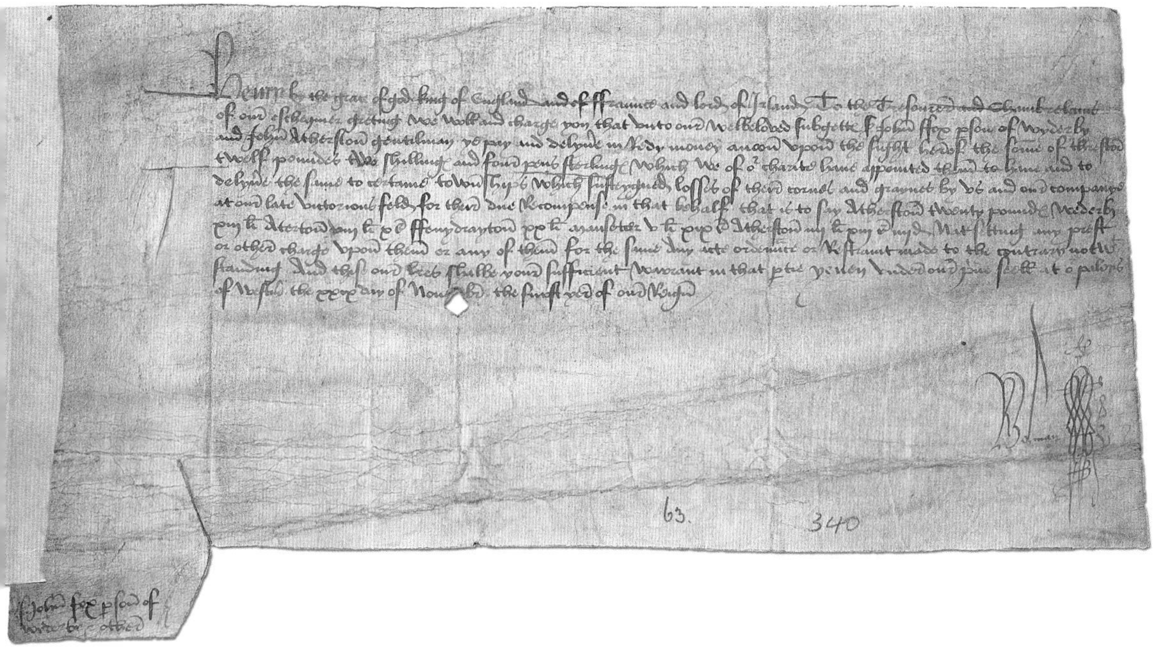

Henry by the grace of god king of England and of ffraunce and lord of Irland. To the Tresourer and Chamberleyns of our Eschequer greting. We wol and charge you that unto our welbeloved subgettes S[ir] John ffitz [illegible] person of Wyderby and John Atherston gentilman ye pay and delyver in redy money anoon upon the sight herof the some of thre score twelf pounds two shillings and foure pens sterlings which we of o[ur] charite have appointed them to have and to delyver the same to certayne townships which sustayned losses of their cornes and graynes by us and our company at our late victorious feld for their due recompense in that behalf that is to say Atherston twenty pounds Wederby [illegible] Atherston [illegible] ffenydrayton [illegible] Mancetter [illegible] Atherston [illegible] without any prest or other charge upon them or any of them for the same any acte ordenance or restraint made to the contrary notwithstanding. And thise our lettres shalbe your sufficient warrant in that partie. Yeven under our prive seell at o[ur] paleys of Westm[inster] the xxx day of Novembre the first yere of our Reigne.

R [illegible]

63. 340

S[ir] John ffitz [illegible] person of Wederby & other

Henry by the grace of god king of England and of ffraunce and lord of Irland. To the Tresourer and Chamberleyns of our Eschequer greting. Where as we verily understand that our right welbeloved in god thabbot of our monastery of Miravall had and sustayned right grete hurte charges and losses by occasion of the grete repaire and resorte that our people commyng toward our late feld made afore unto the house of Mirevale aforesaid as in goyng over his groundes to the destruction of his cornes and pastures. We late you wite that we in recompense of the same have yeven and graunted unto him the some of oon hundreth marc sterlings to be had and paied of o[ur] rewarde. Wherfor we wol and charge you that ye unto the said Abbot make contentacion and payment of the said some of oon hundreth marc in redy money without prest or other charge to be sette upon him for the same. And thise our lettres shalbe your sufficient warrant and discharge ayenst us in that behalf. Yeven under o[ur] prive seel at o[ur] paloys of Westm[inster] the vj day of Decembre the first yere of our Reigne.

62

Lany [illegible]

339

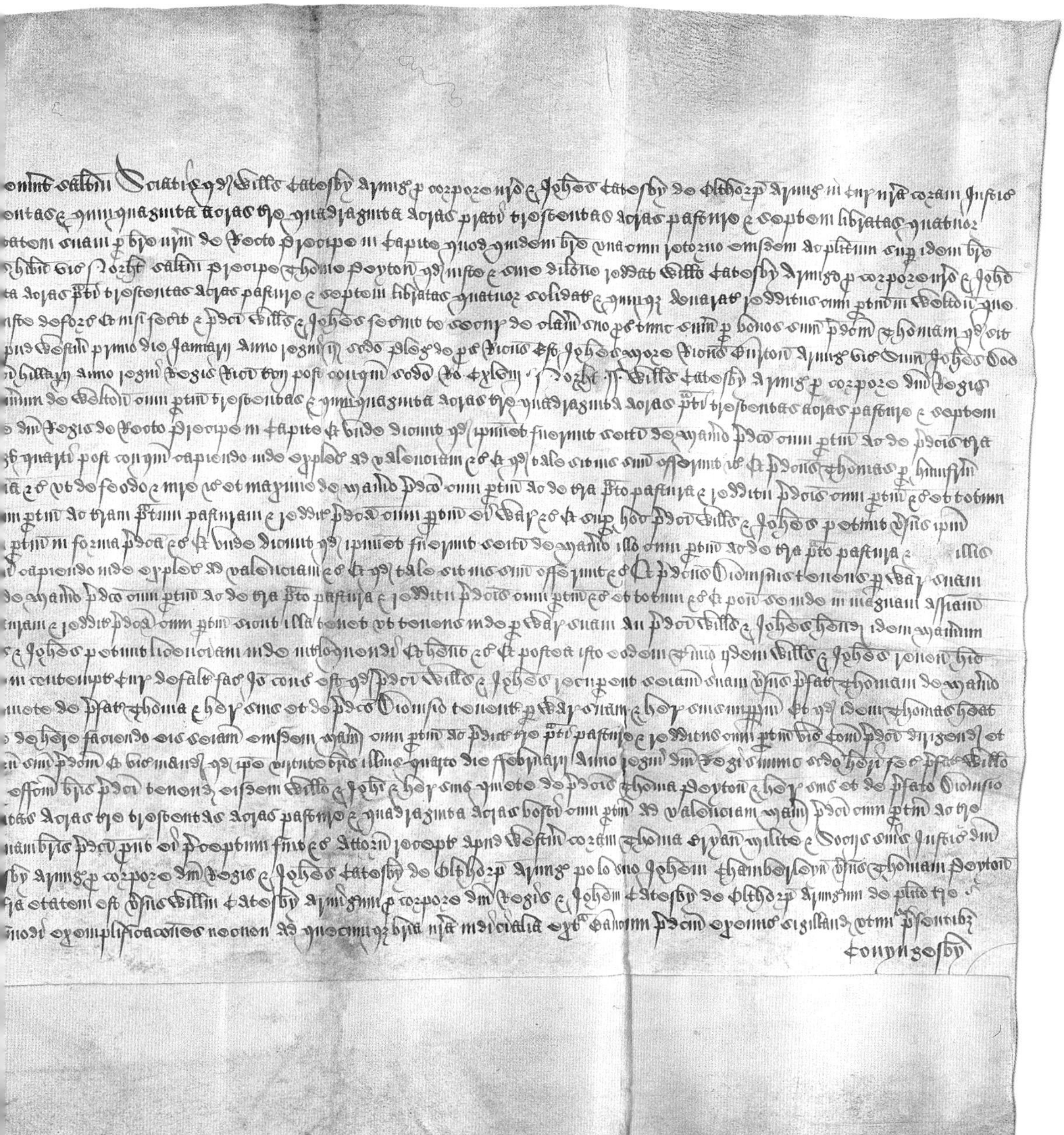

A recovery of the manor of Wetton, Northamptonshire, brought by William Catesby, esquire for the King's body, and John Catesby of Althorp, against Thomas Peyton. The recovery was a legal process to restore a former right to a manor or group of lands by judgement of a court. Many original royal letters patent would have appeared similar to this, with the Great Seal attached at the foot. This obverse face of the seal is shown in greater detail on page 27.

The Seal's reverse shows a shield with the quartered arms of England and France ancient, supported by two of Richard's boars. Henry VII used the same matrix but replaced the boars with Tudor greyhounds.

The French soldiers recruited by Tudor from the military camp at Pont de l'Arche in Normandy were pikemen trained in the latest techniques by expert Swiss captains. These were the troops that made up Tudor's vanguard which engaged the King's leading battle line under the Duke of Norfolk after a brief artillery exchange.

The fighting here was fierce but indecisive. The Stanleys still awaited an advantageous moment to commit themselves. At some point, Richard saw Tudor's standard at the back of his army and, navigating around the main area of fighting, launched a cavalry charge directly at him. Richard attacked without infantry support, calculating that a decisive manoeuvre would kill his rival and immediately end the battle.

This charge was probably made with a large body of the King's personal and household servants. Tudor also may have had recruited more expert mercenaries than we now realize. As a result of Richard's charge, fighting across the battlefield may have slackened as troops awaited the decisive clash of forces. What seems clear from recently re-discovered French sources is that a sufficiently large group of French pikemen were able to retreat and form squares to defend Tudor against Richard's assault. In a highly disciplined and unexpected manoeuvre, never before seen in England, the momentum of Richard's charge was broken and scattered by a wall of pikes.

Richard's main infantry force under Northumberland was now unable to cover the distance from its position to support Richard, since the vanguards of the two armies were between it and the King. This, rather than treachery, may have been the reason why Richard's northern servants, under Northumberland's command, did not join the fighting.

Rubbing of a memorial brass to William Catesby, in Ashby St Ledger church, Northamptonshire.

Catesby was a lawyer and benefited from the local influence of his father in Northamptonshire to secure a good marriage and training at the Inner Temple. His work as legal counsel for the duchy of Lancaster in the midlands brought him powerful clients, connections and an income from which to build his estates. However, his move to Richard's service, through Buckingham and Hastings, was based on his growing political usefulness.

Richard probably dismounted and fought on foot with his closest followers in a desperate effort to reach Tudor. He may have refused a horse to escape the field, and was within feet of Tudor, having killed William Brandon the standard bearer and other men of Tudor's personal bodyguard. This suggests a ferocious contest between equally matched forces. It was as Tudor was about to be struck down that Sir William Stanley's troops poured across the battlefield, overpowered Richard's force and brutally killed the King. Read William Catesby's condemnation of Stanley's actions in document 13, ***Catesby's will.***

The fighting did end almost immediately. Richard's coronet was recovered (reportedly from a thornbush), and his corpse stripped, mutilated and taken to the Greyfriars church at Leicester, where he received a simple burial. At the dissolution of the friary in the 1530s, the tomb was broken and Richard's bones thrown into the river.

# 13 *Catesby's will*

William Catesby's will (in English), written three days after Bosworth in the final hours before his public execution in Leicester. The will indicates Catesby's impressive knowledge of his own landholdings, and also of the complicated arrangement of his titles and estates. It is a curious mixture of practical arrangements, emotive requests and barbed comments about those who will outlive him.

Catesby was one of Richard's leading supporters, and was accused by the King's enemies of having a disproportionate influence within the regime. He and the other members of Richard's 'kitchen cabinet' were lampooned in William Collingbourne's rhyme *The Cat, the Rat and Lovell our Dog, Ruleth all England under a Hog* (Catesby, Sir Richard Ratcliffe and Francis, Lord Lovell ruled second only to Richard himself). Unlike many of Richard's other leading servants, such as Robert Brackenbury and Robert Percy who were killed in the King's final charge at Bosworth, Catesby was captured, perhaps on the battlefield, perhaps skulking at Leicester awaiting news. His reputation as a devious dissembler preceded him, and he was the only leading follower of Richard III to be executed after Bosworth. Had others, such as Lovell or Ratcliffe, been captured they may have met similar swift judgement, but Henry VII needed to use the skills of those Yorkists willing to change allegiance.

Catesby's condemnation, in the final paragraph, of Stanley's behaviour at Bosworth is highly ironical. Both Lord Stanley and Catesby displayed similar behaviour during their careers; both were intent on securing their own positions whatever happened on 22 August 1485. It turned out that Stanley military power, immediately effective in Tudor's favour on the battlefield, was more useful if controlled and wielded from within the new regime, than was Catesby's ability to manipulate the law. Catesby was not given the chance to persuade Henry VII of his usefulness, although the will suggests he would have been quite comfortable transferring his loyalties.

## THE WILL READS:

**First page**

This is the will of William Catesby, esquire, made the 25th day of August the first year of King Henry the VII to be executed by my dear and well-beloved wife [Margaret] to whom I have ever be true of my body, putting my sole trust in her for the execution thereof for the wealth of my soul the which I am undoubted she will execute as for my body, when she may, [it is] to be buried in the church of Ashby St Ledgers, and to do such memorials [prayers] for me as I have appointed by for, and to restore all land that I have wrongfully purchased, and to pay the residue of such land as I have bought truly and to demean [distribute] it among her children and mine as she thinks good after her distraction [grief]. I doubt not the King will be a good and

**Second page**

gracious lord to them [Catesby's children], for he is called a full gracious prince and I never offended him, but my good and free will for God I take to my judge I have ever loved him.

Item that the executors of Nicholas Cowley have the land again in Evertoft without they have their £100.
Item in likewise, Revell his land in Bukley.
Item in likewise, that the copartioners [joint holders of the title to a manor] have their part in Rodinghall in Suffolk if we have right thereto or else to be restored to them that had it before.
Item in likewise the land in Brawnston if the party have right that had it before [if the person who held it previously retains any rights]. And the land besides Kembalton by disposed for my soul and Evertons and so of all other land that the part has right in.
Item that all my father's debts and bequests be executed and paid as to the hove of Catesby and other.
Item that my lady of Buckingham have £100 to help her children and that she will see my lord's debts paid and his will executed. And especially in such land as should be amortised [land alienated in 'mortmain' – conveyed to a corporation] to the hove [use] of Plassly.
Item my lady of Shaftesbury 40 marks.
Item that John Spencer have his £20. And that all other bequests in my other will be executed as my especial trust is in you mistress Margaret [his wife]. And I heartily cry you mercy if I have dealt uncourteously with you. And ever pray you to leave sole and all the days of your life to do for my soul. And their as I have be executors I beseech you see the wills executed. And pray of lord of Winchester my lord of Worcester my lord of London to help you to execute this my will and they will do somewhat for me

And that Richard Frebody may have his £20 again and Bradby £10 or the land at Evertons and you the £10. And I pray you in every place see cleverness in my soul and pray fast [earnestly] and I shall for you and Jesus have mercy upon my soul Amen

My lords Stanley, Strange and all of that blood help and pray for my soul for you have not for my body as I trusted in you. And if my issue receive my land I pray you let master John Elton have the best benefice. And my Lord Lovell come to grace than that you show to him that he pray for me. And uncle John remember my soul as you have done my body and better. And I pray you see the saddler Hartlington be paid and in all other places

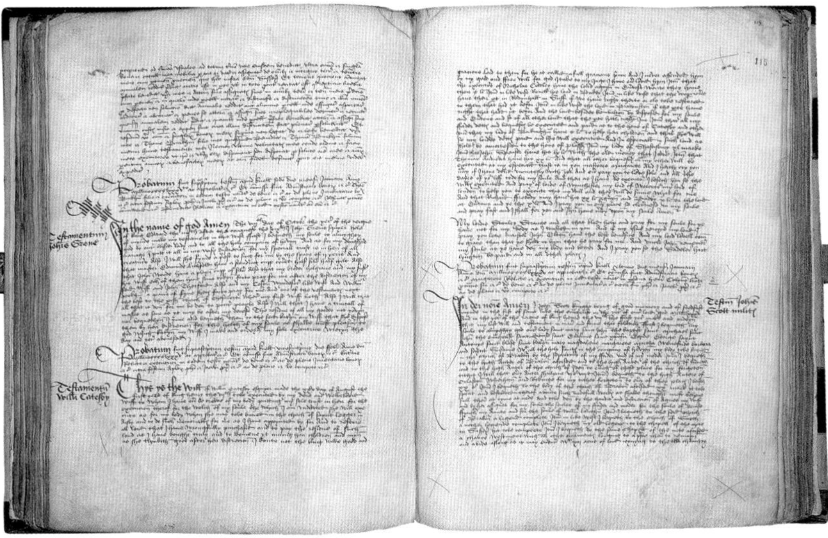

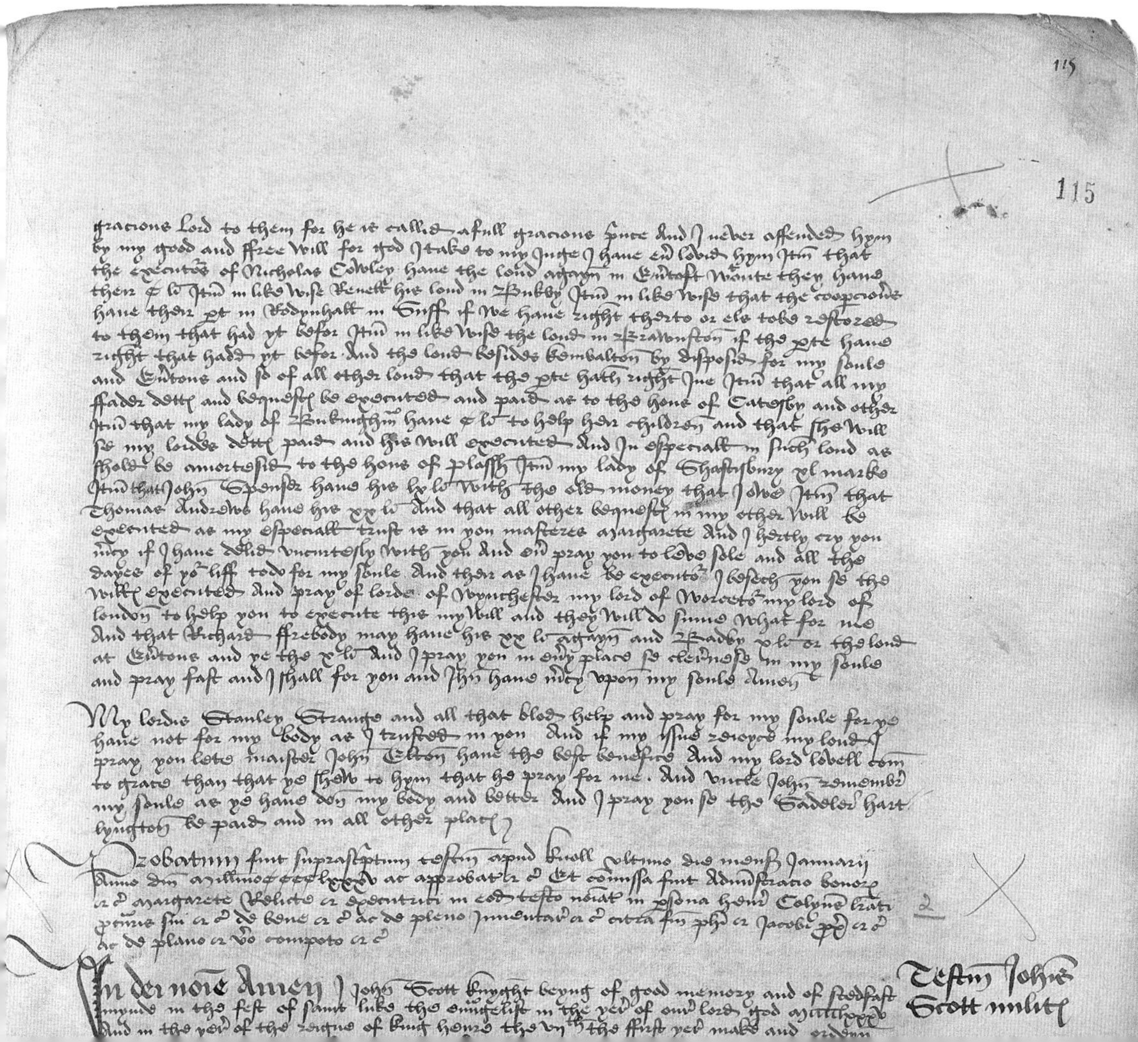

115

115

gracious Lord to them for he is called a full gracious Prince And I never offended hym
by my good and ffree will for god I take to my Juge I have ever loved hym Item that
the executors of Nicholas Cowley have the lond agayn in Enfeld Wrute they have
then x li Item in like wise Revett his lond in Bukby Item in like wise that the cooperode
have ther yt in Bodynhall in Suff if we have right therto or els tobe restored
to them that had yt befor Item in like wise the lond in Brawnston if the pte have
right that hadd yt befor And the lond besides Bombalton by disposid for my soule
and Eydone and so of all other lond that the pte hath right Inne Item that all my
ffader dett and bequest be executed and paid as to the hous of Catesby and other
Item that my lady of Bukingham have c li to help her children and that she will
se my lordes dett paid and his will executed And in especiall in such lond as
shold be amortesid to the hous of Plasshe Item my lady of Shaftesbury xl marke
Item that John Spenser have his x li with the old money that I owe Item that
Thomas Andrewe have his xx li And that all other bequest in my other will be
executed as my especiall trust is in you masteres Margarete And I hertly cry you
mercy if I have delid vncurtesly with you And oft pray you to love sole and all the
dayes of yor liff todo for my soule And ther as I have be executor I beseche you se the
willes executed And pray my lordes of Wynchester my lord of Worcestr my lord of
london to help you to execute this my will and they will do sum what for me
And that Richard ffreebody may have his xx li agayn and Brady x li or the lond
at Eydone and ye the x li And I pray you in euery place se clernesse in my soule
and pray fast and I shall for you and Ihu have mercy vpon my soule Amen

My lordis Stanley Strange and all that blod help and pray for my soule for ye
have not for my body as I trusted in you And if my issue recover my lond I
pray you lete maister John Elton have the best benefice And my lord lovell com
to grace than that ye shew to hym that he pray for me. And Vncle John remembr
my soule as ye have don my body and better And I pray you se the Sadeler hart
lyngton be paid and in all other places

Probatum fuit suprascriptum testum apud Knoll vltimo die mensis Januarij
Anno dni Millmo cccclxxxv at approbat &c Et commissa fuit Administracio bonorum
&c Margarete Relicte &c executrici in eodem testo noiat in persona thome Colyns frati
primis sui &c de bene &c ac de pleno inuentario &c citra fm phi et Jacobi px &c
ac de plano &c vo composito &c

2

In dei noie Amen I John Scott knyght beyng of good memory and of stedfast
mynde in the fest of saint luke the euuangelist in the yer of our lord god Mlcccclxxxv
And in the yer of the reigne of kyng Henre the vii th the ffirst yer make and ordeyn

Testm John
Scott militis

## THE STRENGTH OF RICHARD'S LEGACY, 1485–1509

Henry VII's treatment of Richard III was ignominious, and it did not end support for his memory, nor stifle his legacy. The Tudor King spent seven years unravelling the network of Ricardian and Yorkist support in the north and elsewhere (see document 14, *Loyalty to Richard?*).

The red rose of Lancaster on the King's Bench plea roll (Trinity Term, 1500). Henry Tudor's claim to be heir of Lancaster in 1484 was a dangerous step, forced upon him by the French, which threatened the fragile alliance of support he had gathered about him in exile. In reality, Henry credibly challenged for the Crown because he became a unifying figure. His intention to marry Elizabeth of York and the support of the Yorkist old guard, displaced by Richard's usurpation, promised a restoration of Yorkist rights. His blood relationship to the Lancastrian Beauforts, and to Henry VI himself, revived hopes for Lancastrians, excluded from power since 1471.

A rebellion of Lord Lovell at Easter 1486 almost captured Henry at York. Then in 1487, Richard's nephew John, Earl of Lincoln invaded with Lambert Simnel who was pretending to be Clarence's son Edward, Earl of Warwick. The subsequent Battle of Stoke was almost a re-run of Bosworth, but the Earl of Oxford learned the lessons of August 1485, and gave Henry a comprehensive victory. Lincoln was killed in battle and Lovell disappeared. Henry VII was gradually eliminating the figureheads of Ricardian resistance (see document 15, *Rebellion against Henry*).

A further northern rising occurred in 1489 against the imposition of taxes that Richard had previously abated. The Earl of Northumberland was murdered by rioters, although there were rumours that his leading retainers did not come to his aid in revenge for his failure to fight at Bosworth.

Henry VII's attempt to re-cast the loyalty of the core of Richard's northern support was a calculated risk. The longer he survived unscathed, however, the less likely it became that men like Sir John Conyers and Sir Ralph Bigod would risk their financial security and estates by flirting with rebellion.

# 14 *Loyalty to Richard?*

Bond of allegiance to Henry VII from Sir John Conyers, 11 July 1486. In this document (in Latin), Conyers promises to remain loyal to Henry; the penalty for not doing so is a fine of £2000. The other knights listed are acting as sureties for him, and they stand to forfeit £1000 if the terms of the bond are broken.

This recognizance was taken in the aftermath of the attempt on Henry VII's life at York at Easter 1486. The rebellion was organized by Richard's childhood companion, Francis Lord Lovell and attempted to involve John de la Pole, Earl of Lincoln – nephew and heir of Richard III after 1484, but by then a councillor of the Tudor King, and possibly in the royal party. Conyers' reluctance to confront the rebels implies at least that he was closely monitoring events before declaring his support for the new Tudor power in the north. This could also suggest that Sir John's long-term loyalty to Richard and his political heirs would have re-surfaced had Henry VII been deposed during his first years as King.

Sir John Conyers, as the senior gentry figure of the region, was the effective leader of the surviving members of the old Neville affinity that had transferred their loyalty to Richard of Gloucester after 1471. Others taken to London for interrogation by Henry and his Council were Thomas, James and Brian Metcalfe, Sir Christopher Ward, and William Beverley, Dean of Middleham.

On 13 June 1486 an entry in Henry VII's Council register reports that 'Robin of Riddesdale' was captured in sanctuary in Co. Durham, and was to be brought to London. Given the association of Robin of Redesdale with the Conyers family in 1469, this is perhaps a significant comment, especially as this bond accompanied three others demanded in Chancery at the same time from Christopher, William and Richard Conyers.

These bonds, and others authorized by Henry VII and his Council before the end of 1489, indicate a considerable effort on the part of the new Tudor regime to create stability and to convert the allegiances that had existed in the North Riding since the 1460s. Henry VII's focus on the loyalty of some of Richard's oldest northern retainers does not imply that they had already abandoned their King at Bosworth. If that had been the case, there would have been even less need to establish Tudor authority in the north so swiftly and firmly after 1485.

## THE BOND READS:

Be it remembered that the 11th day of July in the first year of the reign of King Henry VII, Henry, Lord Clifford, knight; Sir John Turbervile, of Southwark, co. Surrey knight; Robert Clifford of London, knight; William Clapham of Westhall, co. York, gentleman; appeared in the presence of the said lord king in his chancery, clearly undertook in person, each of them under pain of £1000 on behalf of John Conyers, knight, and the same John clearly undertook on his own part, under pain of £2000, that the same John shall hereafter bear, hold and govern himself as a faithful liege of the said lord king, and that the same John shall take care not to make nor cause to be made, anything harmful, prejudicial, or injurious to the said lord king in any manner. If it should happen that should John himself hereafter get to know, understand and have foreknowledge of any, treason, conspiracy or any other suspicious material whatsoever prejudicial to the said lord king, that then the said John with all possible haste on his part, and as the occasion shall demand, shall explain, demonstrate and notify the said lord king or his nearest council. And that the same John shall not depart from the city of London without royal authorisation in that respect specifically sought and obtained.

**The enrolled document (bottom) was cut short to save space; the text is completed on the unenrolled version (top):**
... The which sum of £1000 each of the said sureties for himself and the said sum of £2000 the said John, grants to be leviable from their lands and goods to the use of the same lord king if the same John fails to fulfil or to take care to fulfil all the premises in the aforesaid form.

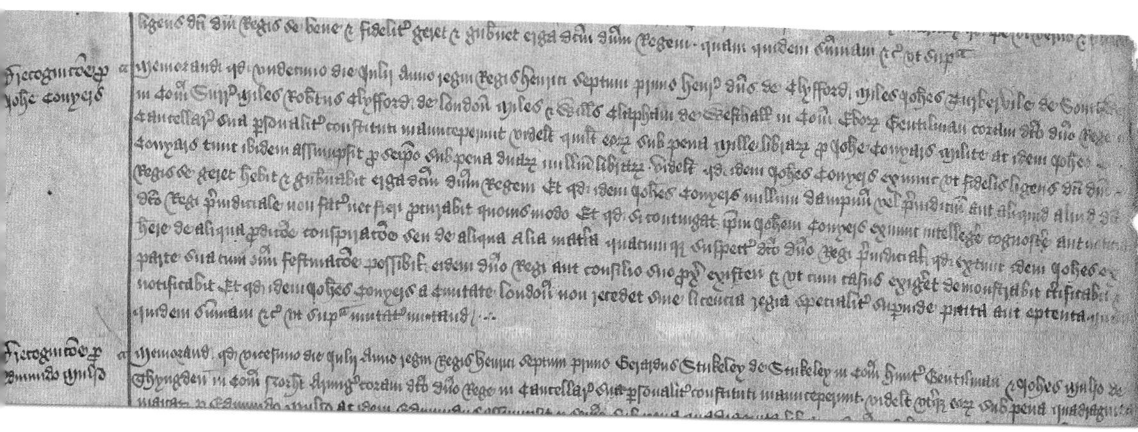

# 15 *Rebellion against Henry*

An Act of Attainder (in English), March 1487. Under this Act, Yorkist rebels forfeited their estates following the rebellion against Henry VII which culminated in the Battle of Stoke.

The leader of the rebels, John de la Pole, Earl of Lincoln, had considerable familiarity with the North Riding as president of Richard's Council of the North. He seems soon to have made his peace with Henry VII, since he was a member of Henry VII's Council by 1486, but was perhaps already plotting for a Yorkist recovery of the Crown. By March 1487 he had fled to Ireland and began to organize the rebellion and invasion of Lambert Simnel.

Historians have speculated as to whether this rising hoped to place Edward, Earl of Warwick on the throne. As the son of Richard's elder brother, Clarence, he had a strong claim to the crown. It is even possible that Lincoln used Simnel and Warwick to disguise his own intentions. Lincoln's brothers Edmund and Richard both claimed the throne in their own right into the mid-Tudor period, so Lincoln may have been hoping that his victory against Henry VII would clear a way for him to seize the Crown.

Lincoln's defection highlighted the difficulties Henry VII faced in imposing himself upon a political elite that had no personal loyalty to him. Henry's exile prevented him developing landed estates and loyal retainers. His followers had congregated around him in opposition to Richard III, and his claims rested upon the position of Elizabeth of York as Edward IV's heir. In amalgamating former loyalties, Henry was vulnerable if the old allegiances of his leading servants could be revived. Lincoln tried this with the pretender Lambert Simnel, but the technique was developed far more effectively during the Perkin Warbeck conspiracy after 1491.

## THE ACT READS:

Forasmuch as the 19th day of the month March last past, John late Earl of Lincoln, nothing considering the great and sovereign kindness that our sovereign liege lord that now is at divers sundry times continually showed to the said late Earl, but that contrary to kind and natural remembrance, his faith truth and allegiance, conspired and imagined the most dolorous and lamentable murder, death, and destruction of the royal person of our said sovereign and liege lord, and also destruction of all this realm, and to perform his said malicious purpose, traitorously departed to the parts beyond the sea, and there accompanied himself with many other false traitors and enemies to our said sovereign liege lord, by long time continuing his malice, prepared a great navy for the coasts of Brabant, and arrived in the ports of Ireland, where he with Sir Henry Bodrugan and John Beaumont, esquire, imagined and conspired the destruction and deposition of our said sovereign liege lord, and for the execution of the same there the 24th day of May last at the city of Dublin, contrary to his homage and faith, truth and allegiance, traitorously renounced, revoked and disclaimed his own said most natural sovereign liege lord and king, and caused one Lambert Simnel, a child of ten years of age, son to Thomas Simnel of Oxford, joiner, to be proclaimed, erected and reputed as king of this realm, and to him did faith and homage to the great dishonour and despite of all this realm. And from thence, continuing in his malicious and traitorous purpose, arrived with a great navy in Furness in Lancashire, the 4th day of June last past, accompanied with a great multitude of strangers with force of arms, that is to say swords, spears, marespikes [morris pikes – pikes supposedly of Moorish origin], bows, guns, harness [plate body armour] brigandines [a padded jacket with a layer of metal plates sewn in], hauberks [a chain-mail tunic], and many other weapons and harness defensible, and from thence the same day, he with...[names of rebels] with many other ill-disposed persons and traitors defensible and in warlike manner arrayed to the number of 8,000 persons, imagining, compassing and conspiring the death and disposition and utter destruction of our said sovereign liege lord the king and subversion of all this realm for the execution and performing of the said mischievous and traitorous purpose, continually in hostile manner passed from thence from place to place to they come to Stoke in the county of Nottingham, where the 16th day of June last past, with banners displayed, levied war against the person of his sovereign and natural liege lord, and gave to him mighty and strong battle, traitorously, contrary to all truth, knighthood, honour, allegiance, faith and affiance, intending utterly to have slain, murdered and cruelly destroyed our said sovereign liege lord and most Christian prince, to the uttermost and greatest adventure of the noble and royal person of our said liege lord, destruction, dishonour and subversion of all this realm. For which malicious, compassed, great, and heinous offence, not only committed against our said sovereign lord, but also against the universal and common weal [welfare] of this realm, is requisite sore and grievous pernicion [wickedness] and also for an example hereafter that none other be bold in likewise to offend. Therefore be it enacted by our sovereign lord the king, by the advice of the lords spiritual and temporal, and the commons in this present parliament assembled, that the said [names of rebels] be reputed, judged and taken as traitors and convicted and attainted of High Treason, etc...

Item quidam actus convictionis et attinctionis certarum personarum in parliamento predicto auctoritate ejusdem parliamenti editus est cum diversis exceptionibus et
provisionibus eidem per prefatum dominum Regem concessis quorum tenores inferius inseruntur et sunt tales.

Actus convictionis et attinctionis

15

Forasmuch as the xix^th^ day of the moneth of Marche last past John late Erle of Lincoln nothyng consideryng the grete and soveraign kyndnes that
oure soveraign liege lorde that nowe is at dyvers sundry tymes contynuelly shewed to the seid late Erle but contrarye to kynd and naturall remembraunce
his feith trouth and allegeaunce conspired and ymagyned the most dolorouse and lamentable murdre deth and distruccion of the royall persone of oure
seid soveraign and liege lorde and also destruccion of all this realme and to performe his seid malicious purpose traiterously departed to the parties beyond
the see and ther accompanyed hym selfe with many other false traitours and enemyes to oure seid soveraign liege lorde by longe tyme
contynuyng his malyce passed a grete navye frome the costes of Flaunders and arryved in the portes of Irland where he with Sir Henry Bodrugan
and John Beaumond squyer ymagyned and conspired the destruccion and deposicion of oure seid soveraign liege lorde and for the execucion of the same
ther the xxiiij day of May last passed at the cite of Develyn contrarie to his homage and feith trouth and allegeaunce traiterously renounced
revoked and disclaymed his same seid most naturall soveraign liege lorde the kyng and caused oone Lambert Symnell a child of x yere of
age sonne to Thomas Symnell late of Oxforde joynour to be proclaymed erecte and reputed as kyng of this realme and to hym did feith and
homage to the grete dishonour and dispite of all this realme and frome thens contynuyng in his malicious and traiterous purpose arryved with a grete
navie in Furnes in Lancasshire the iiij^th^ day of June last past accompanyed with a grete multitude of straungers with force and armes that
is to sey swerdes speres marespikes bowes gonnes harneys brigaundynes hawberkes and many other wepyns and harneis defensible and frome
thens the same day he with Sir Thomas Broughton knyght Thomas Haryngton Robert Percy of Knaresburgh in the countie of Yorke Richard
Harleston John a Broughton brother unto the seid Sir Thomas Broughton knyght Thomas Batell James Haryngton Edward Frank Richard
Mydelton squyers Robert Hilton Clement Skelton Alexander Apilby Richard Banke Edmunde Juse Thomas Blanderhasset gentilmen John Mallary of
Lichebarowe in the countie of Northampton Robert Mallary of Fallesley in the same countie Gyles Mallary of Grenysnorton in the same countie William
Mallary of Stowe in the same countie Robert Mannyng late of Dunstaple William Kay of Halyfax gentilman Roger Hartlyngton Richard
Hoggesson John Abyntry Rouland Robynson yomen with many other ill disposed persones and traytours defensible and in like wise arrayed in manere
of werre to the nombre of viij^m^ persones ymagynyng compassyng and conspiryng the deth and deposicion and utter destruccion of oure seid soveraign
liege lorde the kyng and the subversion of all this realme for the execucion and performyng of the seid mystherous and traiterous purpose contynuelly
in hostyle maner passed fro thens from place to place to they come to Stoke in the countie of Notyngham where the xvj day of June last
past with baners displayed levied werre ayenst the persone of his soveraign and naturall liege lorde and gave to hym myghty and stronge batell
traiterously and contrarie to all trouth knyghthode honour allegeaunce feith and affyaunce intendyng utterly to have sleyne murdred and
cruelly destroyed oure forseid liege lorde and most cristen prynce to the uttermost and grettest aventure of the noble and royall persone of oure seid
liege lorde destruccion dishonour and subversion of all this realme For the which malicious compassed grete and heynous offence not all
oonly commytted ayen oure seid soveraign lorde but also ayenst the universall and comen wele of this realme yt requyreth sore and grevous
punycion and also for an example hereafter that non other be bold in like wise to offend Therfor be it enacted by oure soveraign lorde the kyng
by the advyse of all the lordes spirituell and temporall and the comens in this present parliament assembled and by the auctorite of the same that the
seid John late Erle of Lincoln Sir Henry Bodrugan Thomas Broughton knyghtes John Beaumond Thomas Haryngton Robert Percy
Richard Harleston John a Broughton Thomas Batell James Haryngton Edward Frank Richard Mydelton squyers Robert Hilton Clement
Skelton Alexander Apylby Richard Banke Edmunde Juse Thomas Blanderhasset gentilmen John Mallary of Lichebarowe in the countie of Northampton Robert
Mallary of Fallesley in the same countie Gyles Mallary of Grenysnorton in the same countie William Mallary of Stowe in the same countie Robert
Mannyng late of Dunstaple William Kay of Halyfax gentilman Roger Hartlyngton Richard Hoggesson Rouland Robynson John Abyntry
yomen be reputed, jugged and taken as traitours and convicte and attaynte of high treason and that all honours castelles lordshippes maners hundredes
londes and tenementes with ther appurtenaunces advousons knyghtes fees feefermes remayndres reversions liberties letes jurisdiccions fraunchises and other
hereditamentes goodes and catalles whiche the seid late Erle Thomas Blanderhasset Thomas Batell and Edmunde Juse or eny of theym or eny
other to the use of theym or eny of theym hadde or were possessed of eny estate of enheritaunce the xix day of Marche last past be forfeite to oure
soveraign lorde the kyng to have and to hold to hym and to his heires for ever And that all honours castelles lordshippes maners hundredes londes and tenementes
with ther appurtenaunces advousons knyghtes fees feefermes remayndres reversions liberties letes jurisdiccions and other hereditamentes goodes
and catalles which the seid Sir Henry Bodrugan and John Beaumond or either of theym or eny other to their use or the use of either of theym
hadde the xx^ti^ day of Novembre the secund yere of the reigne of the kyng that nowe is be forfeite to the kyng to have and enjoye to hym and
to his heires for ever And that all honours castelles lordshippes maners hundredes londes and tenementes with ther appurtenaunces advousons knyghtes
fees feefermes remayndres reversions liberties letes jurisdiccions fraunchises and other hereditamentes goodes and catalles which the seid Thomas Broughton
Thomas Haryngton Robert Percy Richard Harleston John a Broughton James Haryngton Edward Frank Richard Mydelton Robert Hylton
Clement Skelton Alexander Apilby Richard Banke John Mallary of Lychebarowe in the countie of Northampton Robert Mallary of Fallesley in the same
countie Gyles Mallary of Grenysnorton William Mallary of Stowe in the same countie Robert Mannyng late of Dunstaple William Kay
of Halyfax gentilman Roger Hartlyngton Richard Hoggesson Rouland Robynson and John Abyntry or eny of theym or eny other to their use
or to the use of eny of theym had or was possessed of of eny estate of enheritaunce the iiij day of June last past be forfeite to the kyng to have
and enjoye to hym and to his heires for ever And also be it ordeygned and establisshed by the seid advyse assent and auctorite that yf the seid persones by
this acte attaynted have made eny estate feoffement or discontynuaunce of eny londes tenementes rentes possessions or other hereditamentes wherof they
be or eny of theym were seised or possessed in the right of eny of their wifes at the tyme of such estate feoffementes or discontynuaunces made
to eny persone or persones in eny wise that the seid londes tenementes rentes possessions and heretamentes be not comprised in this acte but utterly be excepted
and forprised out of the same and that right and title of eny of the seid wyfes of and in all such londes tenementes rentes possessions and other hereditamentes
be and rest in eny of the seid wifes and they to be at ther accions and recoveres of the same and eny parcell therof accordyng to the course of the comen
[illegible] in this present parliament made or to be made not withstondyng And also that yt be lefull

**Perkin Warbeck**

Warbeck was the son of a boatman from Tournai in Belgium, yet with careful coaching and brilliant acting he was able to impersonate the youngest of the Princes in the Tower, Richard, Duke of York, for eight years after 1491. His tale of escape from the Tower caused astonishment around Europe. Because of his apparent intimate knowledge of Edward IV's son, Warbeck retained the support and protection of Richard's sister Margaret, dowager Duchess of Burgundy, the Emperor Maximilian and James IV of Scotland. He even married a kinswoman of James, Lady Katherine Gordon. We shall never know whether these European royals wholly believed Warbeck's story, or if he was a convenient pawn in shifting European politics at the beginning of the Habsburg-Valois wars over Italy. Either way, he caused major concern for the Tudor Crown in England and almost cost Henry VII his throne in 1497. Warbeck was hanged in 1499.

After 1489, the King even placed Thomas, Earl of Surrey at the head of the Council of the North. Surrey had fought with his father, Norfolk, against Tudor at Bosworth. His rehabilitation provided an example that few former Ricardians in the north ignored. By 1492 a final murmur of discontent at Ackworth near Pontefract was dispersed with barely a mention in official documents.

However, Henry VII remained vulnerable. In 1492, Perkin Warbeck claimed to be Richard, Duke of York, miraculously smuggled from the Tower in 1483. Warbeck's appearance split the allegiance of the loyal Yorkists who had flocked to Tudor after October 1483. This was a national crisis that struck at the heart of Henry VII's government, and it immediately undermined Tudor credibility. The steward of the household, Lord Fitzwalter, truly believed Warbeck to be

Prince Richard, and plotted on his behalf. Even Henry's Chamberlain, Sir William Stanley, stated that he could not oppose Warbeck if the claim were true. For this uncertainty, Stanley was executed in 1495.

It took Henry many years to subdue this conspiracy. Another south-western rebellion in 1497 was finally crushed at the gates of London on Blackheath. Yet even when Warbeck was finally executed in 1499, Henry drove another of Richard III's nephews, Edmund de la Pole, Earl of Suffolk, into exile and conspiracy. Suffolk's capture in 1506 finally ended the dynastic threat against Henry VII, but by then Henry was prematurely aged and sickly. The succession of Henry VIII in 1509 had to be carefully orchestrated by the surviving Tudor old guard from 1483. Richard III's legacy would continue to have a lasting effect.

The monument of Thomas Lord Stanley, 1st Earl of Derby, and his first wife, Eleanor Neville, in Ormskirk Church, Lancashire. Between 1471 and 1500, the Stanleys were the effective kingmakers within England. Their dominance of the north-west gave them the manpower to raise large forces during the crises of the reigns of Edward IV, Richard III and Henry VII. Stanley neutrality was often as effective as the intervention of other lords, and their direct involvement at Bosworth helped to establish the Tudor dynasty.

# The Real Richard III: Man or Myth?

## THE STRENGTH OF FAMILY

The idea that Richard was immoral or evil is found in the earliest stories of his life and reign. Much of this stems from Tudor assertions that a king who murdered his own nephews can have had no moral basis to his personality. All of his apparently benevolent actions or proclamations of good lordship were therefore shallow pretence and showmanship, designed to win the hearts and minds of his subjects. However, there is evidence that this was not entirely true.

Richard was undoubtedly a cultured religious benefactor. Many of his ten religious college or chantry chapel foundations occurred before he became King. His intended colleges at Middleham and Barnard Castle were major projects. In the 1478 foundation statutes of Middleham, there is a strong sense of Richard's personal devotion, and his choice of saints, including Ninian and Cuthbert, suggests a deep understanding of popular northern piety.

The weekly requiem Mass Richard required to be held for his late father was also unusual and implies a permanent devotion to his father's memory, the legacy of which later emerged in Richard's claim to the throne. Richard can hardly have remembered his father, so it seems likely that it was Cecily who maintained his legacy to their son. In 1484 Richard praised the 'manifold benevolent services' that James, Earl of Desmond's father had shown to the Duke of York in Ireland in 1459. Since Richard was only five years old when York was exiled, this may have been knowledge that Cecily passed on to him.

The 'broken sword' portrait of Richard III (see also p. 96).

Richard, who physically resembled his father, took a prominent role as chief mourner at York's reburial at Fotheringhay in 1476, and he may have used his father's military code as a model. In the late 1470s Richard drew up the ordnances for the heralds and provided for them a house in London that became the College of Arms. His interest in a chivalric code of conduct was recognized by Caxton, who dedicated a printing of Ramon Lull's *Order of Chivalry* to the King.

Part of Caxton's enthusiasm for Richard's chivalry was the King's interest in a crusade, which was voiced to Nicholas von Popplau, a German visitor to the court in 1484. Recent research has identified a strong crusading zeal in Richard's self-image, and it has been suggested that this ideal may have been intended as a major act of contrition for the manner of his accession. Alternatively, it could be a further example of Richard demonstrating to his subjects his intention to assume the highest form of duty for a Christian king.

If Richard of York's legacy guided Richard's chivalric and martial deeds, then in his religious benefactions the King had a strong role model in the person of his mother, who supported institutions at Fotheringhay, Clare and Syon throughout her life. Richard's relationship with Cecily also went much deeper than Shakespeare's characterization suggests. Few letters between the King and his mother have survived, but it is interesting that one written in 1474 and another from 1484 are similar in tone, indicating a personal understanding, respect, and pleasure in each other's company (see document 16, ***'Most humble son'***).

Cecily had a prominent role in the events of 1483, when her house was both the venue for crucial meetings and a base for her son. Her relationship with Richard seems to have continued on amicable

Rubbing of a memorial brass to Elizabeth 'Jane' Shore from her parents' memorial at Hinxsworth, Herts. Elizabeth had been mistress to Edward IV, William Lord Hastings, Thomas, Marquis of Dorset, and Thomas Lynom (Richard's solicitor, who secured her release from prison after she had performed her penance through London's streets). Her influence over these men, and the political consequences of her liaisons, made her a target for Richard's moralizing. However, Sir Thomas More's sympathetic description of her suggests that she was more of a victim than a political manipulator.

terms after Edward V was deposed, suggesting that she broadly agreed with her son's actions, even though they fractured the family that she headed.

Cecily's probable later involvement in plotting against Henry VII, and the somewhat ironical bequests to the Tudors in her will (including a bed carved with the wheel of fortune to Henry VII's heir Arthur, Prince of Wales), may imply her bitterness at the fact and nature of Richard's death. This was not the reaction of a mother opposed to the manner of her son's accession.

## RICHARD'S MORALITY

This aspect of Richard's personality is very difficult to quantify. In the *Titulus Regius* he strongly condemned the dissolute living of the Woodvilles and the wilfulness of his lecherous brother Edward IV. He targeted Elizabeth Shore, who had been mistress to both Edward and Lord Hastings, and made her perform public penance as a harlot. Proclamations denouncing Henry Tudor alleged all kinds of immoral intentions, with emphasis on his illegitimate Beaufort blood, and Richard's letter, of 1484, to all the bishops affirmed his wish to see virtuous living advanced.

# 16 'Most humble son'

A letter from Richard to his mother, 3 June 1484, sent from Pontefract.

This letter (in English) is one of a very few to survive between Richard III and his mother Cecily Neville, Duchess of York. No reply is known. It could therefore represent something of a one-sided correspondence, with Richard attempting to improve things with his mother after his usurpation. Richard's plea that his mother may write often for his comfort could suggest that she has not done so frequently before. However, other parts of the text suggest that they have been in regular communication following the death of the Prince of Wales two months earlier. Richard's request that Viscount Lovell be made the Duchess's receiver (*i.e.* an agent to manage her estates) in Wiltshire is not a forceful instruction, nor something that Richard could have hoped to influence had Cecily been hostile.

Cecily's prompting had been able to rein-in Richard when his tenants clashed with Cecily's officers in 1474, at the height of his rise as Duke of Gloucester. Surviving records do not offer much evidence of personal visits, but Cecily becomes more prominent during Richard's quest for the throne, when the York family house in London, Baynards Castle, was used for important meetings and was the place where Richard accepted the Crown on 25 June.

After Richard's death, Cecily championed her de la Pole grandchildren, and may have supported John, Earl of Lincoln's rebellion in 1487. Her household servants were involved with Perkin Warbeck's conspiracy when the Duchess died in 1495. This evidence suggests that she believed in the right of the York family to rule England, and that Richard III was still considered as part of that family. It has even been suggested recently that Cecily had a central and direct role in bringing about Edward V's deposition to restore what she considered to be the legitimate Yorkist line.

## RICHARD'S LETTER READS:

Madam, I recommend me to you as heartily as is to me possible. Beseeching you in most humble and affectionate wise [way] of your daily blessing to my singular comfort and defence in my need. And madam, I heartily beseech you that I may often hear from you to my comfort. And such news as has been here, my servant Thomas Brayne this bearer shall show you, to whom please it you to give credence unto. And madam I beseech you to be a good and gracious lady to my Lord Chamberlain [Lovell] to be your officer in Wiltshire in such as Collingbourne had. I trust he shall therein do you good service. And that it please you that by this bearer I may understand your pleasure in this behalf. And I pray God send you the accomplishment of your noble desires. Written at Pontefract the 3rd day of June with the hand of

Your most humble son<br>
Richard rex

Madam I recommaunde me to you as hertely as is to me possible
Beseching you in my most humble ~~wise~~ and effectuouse wise of
yor daly blissing to my Synguler comfort & defense in my nede
And madam I hertely beseche you that I may often here from you to my
comfort / And suche newes as bey here ~~here~~ my servaunt Thomas
Bryan this berer shall shewe you / to whome please it you to yeve
credence unto / And madam I beseche you to be good & gracious
lady to my lord my Chamberleyn to be yor officer in Wilshire in suche
as Colingbourne had / I trust he shall therin do you good service
And that it please you that by this berer I may understande your
pleasur in this behalve / And I pray god sende you thaccomplisshement
of yor noble desires / Written at Pountfreit the iijde day of Juyn
with the hande of

Ao 1484
Ao Reg. 2

Yor most humble son
Ricardus Rex

A grotesque carved wooden head of Richard III from a choir stall. Many of the images of Richard created after 1485 reflected Tudor allegations of his deformities and cruel nature.

Much of this evidence might be dismissed merely as a re-invention of his reasons for taking the throne. By contrasting his conduct with the vices of previous powerful figures, Richard presented himself as a highly principled, almost prurient monarch, apparently determined to rule from the moral high ground. But there may have been a deeper intent behind the frequent assertion of this kind of message.

Richard was faced with an enemy who would not show himself until ready. Until that time, a steady stream of support was slipping away to join Tudor. Richard's reign therefore appeared ever more like a northern imposition on the rest of the country. In seeking ways to undermine Tudor's credibility, Richard tried to balance a broadening of his appeal with maintenance of his professed intention for moral government.

This predicament is seen in April 1485 when, after the death of Queen Anne, his former Neville supporters effectively forced Richard to deny publicly that he intended to marry his niece, Elizabeth of York. Such a marriage made sound sense as a measure to undermine Tudor, but it also threatened the new national authority of Richard's longest serving followers, since it invited a return of the Woodvilles.

The manner of Anne's death, and Richard's reported unwillingness to visit her (she may have died from tuberculosis), led to rumours that she was poisoned to make possible the political marriage with Elizabeth. If Richard really did intend to marry Elizabeth, he thereby tacitly acknowledged either that she was legitimate and therefore carried real dynastic importance, or that he was prepared to marry his own niece simply to defeat Tudor. The former is unlikely: even if the pre-contract story were true, Eleanor Butler had died in 1468. If Edward IV and Elizabeth Woodville had then performed a second marriage ceremony, the Princes, who were born after that date, would have been legitimate, but Elizabeth of York who arrived in 1466, would still have been considered a bastard. This makes Richard's alleged intention to marry her appear to be a desperate expedient to confound Henry Tudor. Such a union was well outside accepted degrees of blood relationship, and stood contrary to Richard's repeated message of 'clean-living', but to many Tudor writers was proof of his immorality.

The fact that the King had two acknowledged illegitimate children did not help his credibility. The eldest, Katherine, married one of Richard's allies, William Herbert, in 1484. John of Gloucester was younger and still a minor when made Captain of Calais in March 1485. Both children were likely to have been conceived before Richard's marriage (see document 17, ***John of Gloucester***).

Assessment of Richard's morality is extremely difficult. His use of character assassination and defamation makes it hard to separate Richard's public presentation of himself from the private feelings he must have held. The Tudor vilification of Richard III only compounds this problem.

## RICHARD III'S REPUTATION

Many historians now accept that the true image of Richard has been distorted by the Tudor interpretation of his life. Even Dominic Mancini's report, written

# 17 *John of Gloucester*

The first document (in Latin) records the appointment of Richard's illegitimate son, John of Gloucester, as Captain of Calais, 11 March 1485. The second document (in English) shows a payment to John for this role, although the sum was not accounted until Henry VII's reign – not surprisingly, John was replaced as Captain after Bosworth. Very little else is known of his life.

The positive language of this grant to Richard's illegitimate son is unusual and intriguing. After the death of the Prince of Wales, John of Gloucester was Richard's only acknowledged surviving son. This may account for the fatherly hopes for future personal and dynastic service that Richard expressed. Despite his illegitimacy, John was very much part of the Yorkist family, and the King champions his physical abilities, mental qualities and, tellingly, his interest in virtuous rule though his 'inclination to all good customs'. The captaincy of Calais was vitally important for national security, Calais having been held and exploited by Warwick and Hastings during earlier periods. Therefore, John was being prepared for a major role in Richard's regime; however, the illegitimacy of John, and his half-sister Katherine, was not a threat to the Yorkist dynasty because their births did not arise from adultery within royal marriage.

John's preparation for such a role matches that achieved by Arthur Plantagenet, a bastard of Edward IV, who held office at Calais under Henry VIII (his maternal nephew). King Henry's own natural son, Henry Fitzroy (b. 1519), was given the royal title of Duke of Richmond and the Lancastrian dukedom of Somerset, closely aligning himself with the Tudors' Lancastrian inheritance. He also resided at Sheriff Hutton and led the Council of the North until his early death in July 1536. At that time he was Henry VIII's only surviving male child. Both of these royal bastards were major political figures who held strategic office. It is likely that Richard shared the view of many continental rulers that illegitimate royal children, who posed no threat to the Crown or to the succession, could be a source of loyalty and stability for a monarch.

## THE GRANT READS:

The king to all to whom &c, greeting. Among all, our well-beloved bastard son, John of Gloucester, whose disposition and natural vigour, agility of body and inclination to all good customs, promises us by divine grace, great and certain hope of future service. Know that we by our special grace, and out of certain knowledge and our mere motion, ordain and appoint the same John captain of our town and castle of Calais and of our Tower of Rysbank and our Lieutenant in the Marches of the same. Excepting and reserving wholly to us the gift and grant of offices during the minority of the same John, before he reaches the age of 21 years. Having, occupying and exercising the posts of Captain and Lieutenant aforesaid, the said John himself or through his sufficient deputy or deputies from the fourth day of March last past for the term of his life with all rights, honours, and profits, fees, wages, rewards and prerogatives, in all full power and form according as any other captain of the said town had before this time, excepting and reserving as is aforesaid...

## THE PAYMENT:

... Also of money paid to the said late King Richard and John of Gloucester his son and captain of the said town [of Calais] and the soldiers of the same £5723, 18s, 9d ...

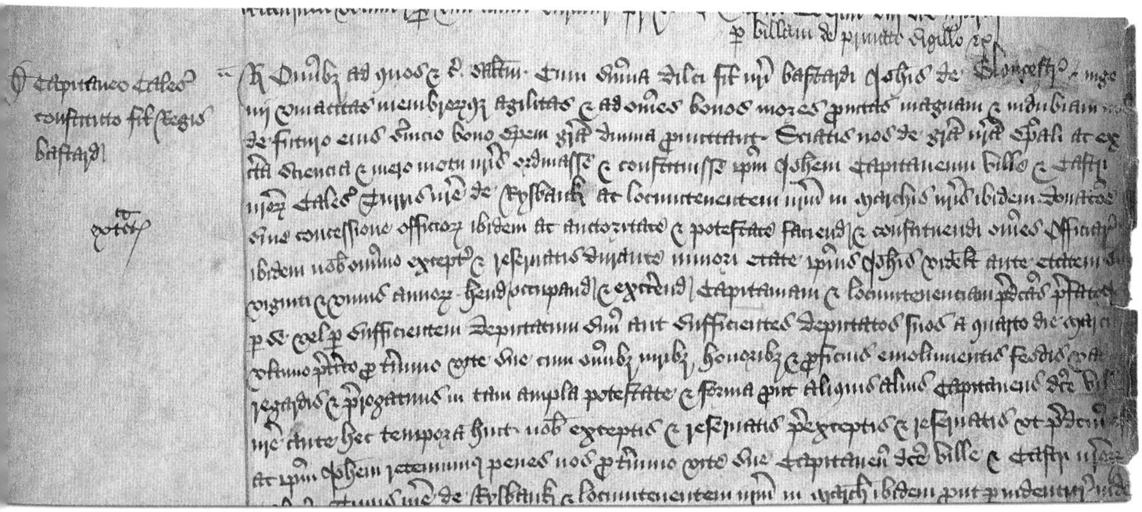

per billetum de priuato sigillo [illegible]

De Capitaneo Calesie constituto filio Regis bastardo

Ricardus etc. Omnibus ad quos etc. salutem. Cum dilectus filius noster bastardus Johannes de Gloucestre [illegible] ... [illegible]

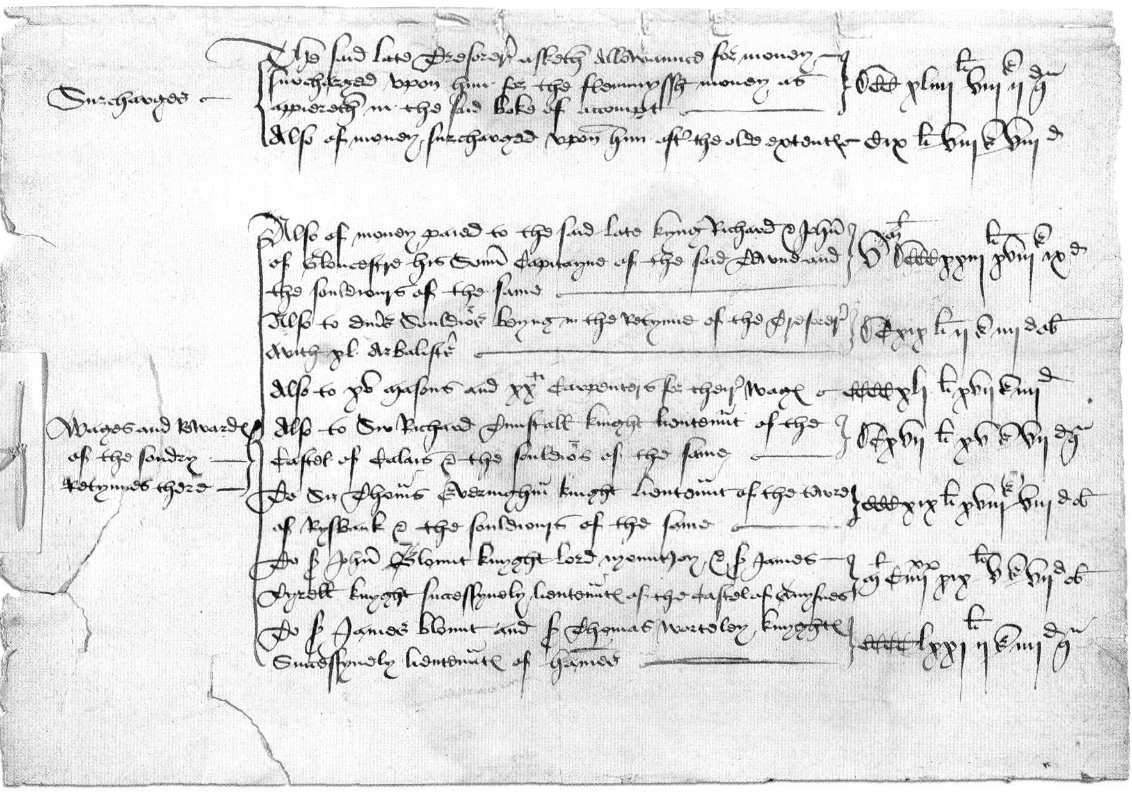

Surcharges — The said late Tresorer askyth allowaunce for money surcharged upon him for the Flemyssh money as apperith in the said boke of acompt [illegible]

Also of money surcharged upon him of the old extente [illegible]

Wages and Rewardes of the soudiers retynues there —

Also of money paied to the said late kyng Richard & John of Gloucestre his sonne Capitayne of the said Towne and the souldiours of the same [illegible]

Also to dyvers souldiours beyng in the retynue of the Tresorer [illegible] pl. Arbalestr [illegible]

Also to the masons and xx^ti carpenters for their wages [illegible]

Also to Sir Richard Tunstall knyght lieutenaunt of the Castel of Calais & the souldiours of the same [illegible]

To Sir Thomas Mountgomery knyght lieutenaunt of the towre of Rysbank & the souldiours of the same [illegible]

To Sir John Blount knyght lord Mountjoy & Sir James Tyrell knyght successyvely lieutenauntes of the Castel of Guynes [illegible]

To Sir James Blount and Sir Thomas Wortley knyghtes successyvely lieutenauntes of Hammes [illegible]

in the summer of 1483, may have relied on rumours among foreign merchants in London, and the views of former servants of Edward IV and V. This perhaps made his observations as subjective as accounts written after Bosworth.

The 'broken sword' portrait of Richard III, probably made during the final decade of Henry VIII's reign. The sword suggests Richard's shattered authority. The x-ray (right) of the portrait reveals deformity of the left hand and a crude hump painted onto the left shoulder.

However, some unbiased reports of Richard and his reign do exist. Nicholas von Popplau wrote a memoir of his visit to court in 1484, which includes his impressions of Richard. He does not mention any of the King's physical defects alleged by Tudor writers, such as uneven shoulders or deformity of the arms. A version of the roll of John Rous written before 1485 is positive about Richard's abilities (see document 18, ***Richard's image***); this work was re-written from a Tudor perspective after Richard's death. There is also surviving evidence from the King's servants, such as a eulogistic note on Richard's abilities by Robert Stillington, Bishop of Bath and Wells in 1483, or the enthusiastic responses in the north to the progress of the King and Queen that same year.

These and other works are but brief sketches of Richard. Many emphasize his potential to be a great king, but the authors perhaps hoped to cultivate royal favour, making it difficult to find objectivity in English commentaries on Richard before 1485. However, the post-Bosworth evidence not only blatantly obscures the true nature of Richard III, it still dominates the popular historical assessment of him. These sources are often literary histories, constructed to offer allegorical and instructive advice to Tudor audiences.

## SHAKESPEARE AND THE TUDOR VIEW OF RICHARD

The strongest modern view of Richard III is still that developed by William Shakespeare. This is the familiar image of the duplicitous, hunchbacked conspirator, willing to use any means to gain the Crown. Shakespeare's main sources for Richard's character and actions were Polydore Vergil's *Anglica Historia* and Sir Thomas More's *History of King Richard III.*

Vergil worked on his *Historia* after 1506 when he became an employee of the first two Tudor kings. He sifted the recollections of those that brought Henry VII to power, making his work a mixture of official Tudor history and direct propaganda. More's work was primarily an investigation of tyranny, and a

# 18 *Richard's image*

Pencil drawings, with heraldic crests, family coats of arms, eulogies and descriptions of Richard III, his wife Anne Neville and their son, Edward, Prince of Wales, from the *Rous Roll.*

The *Rous Roll* is one of England's late medieval treasures. It is a visual representation of the descent of the Earls of Warwick and was compiled by John Rous, a Warwickshire antiquary and chantry priest, to accompany his *History of the Kings of England.* Rous wrote this English version of the roll, now in the British Library, during Richard's reign before the death of Edward, Prince of Wales in April 1484. It is fulsome in its praise Richard's abilities, although Anne Neville, as daughter of an Earl of Warwick, gets a longer entry. In his description of Richard's descent in the male line without discontinuance or defiling, Rous echoed the King's own assertion in the *Titulus Regius* that he was the true heir of Richard, Duke of York.

At some point towards the end of Richard's reign, however, Rous began to re-write the *History* and he also re-drafted the illustrations and descriptions. Richard then became scorpion-like, with a smooth front and stinging tail. He was born deformed after two years in the womb, and murdered not only his nephews, but also his wife Anne, and King Henry VI. Richard was erased from the illustration, and was replaced by Anne's first husband Edward, son of Henry VI. The earlier praise of Richard's legal reforms and the love that his subjects bore him was also removed. Rous evidently could not get possession of his original roll after 1485, and it has survived to indicate the severity of his changed opinion of Richard. Rous undoubtedly wrote with his immediate audience and royal master in mind, and both of his descriptions of Richard perhaps reflected this.

## JOHN ROUS WROTE:

**Anne Neville**

The most noble lady and princess, born of the royal blood of diverse realms, lineally descending from princes, kings, emperors and many glorious saints, dame Anne, by the great provision of God, Queen of England, of France, and Lady of Ireland. Wife first unto Prince Edward, son and heir to King Henry the sixth, and after his decease, marvellously conveyed by all the corners and parts of the wheel of fortune and soon exalted again higher than ever she was to the most high throne and honour over all other ladies of this noble realm anointed and crowned Queen of England, wife unto the most victorious prince King Richard the third. In person she was seemly, amenable and beauteous, and in conditions full commendable and right virtuous. And according to the interpretation of her name Anne, full gracious. She was second daughter and one of the heirs of the most mighty and noble lord Sir Richard Neville, Earl of Warwick and Salisbury, and his worshipful lady and wife dame Anne. This most noble princess was born in the castle of Warwick the 11th day of the month of June the year of our Lord 1456, and in our lady church there with great solemnity was she christened.

**Richard III**

The most mighty prince Richard by the grace of God King of England and of France and Lord of Ireland; by very matrimony without discontinuance of any defiling in the law by heir male lineally descending from King Henry the second; all avarice set aside, ruled his subjects in his realm full commendably, punishing offenders of his laws, especially extortioners and oppressors of his commons, and cherishing those that were virtuous, by which discreet guiding he got great thanks of God and love of all his subjects, rich and poor, and great laud [praise] of the people of all other lands about him.

**Prince Edward**

The noble and mighty prince, Edward, Prince of Wales, Duke also of Cornwall and Earl of Chester. Son and heir to the most high and mighty prince King Richard the third and his most noble lady and wife Queen Anne. Inheritor to both royal possessions, he was born in the castle of Middleham in the north country.

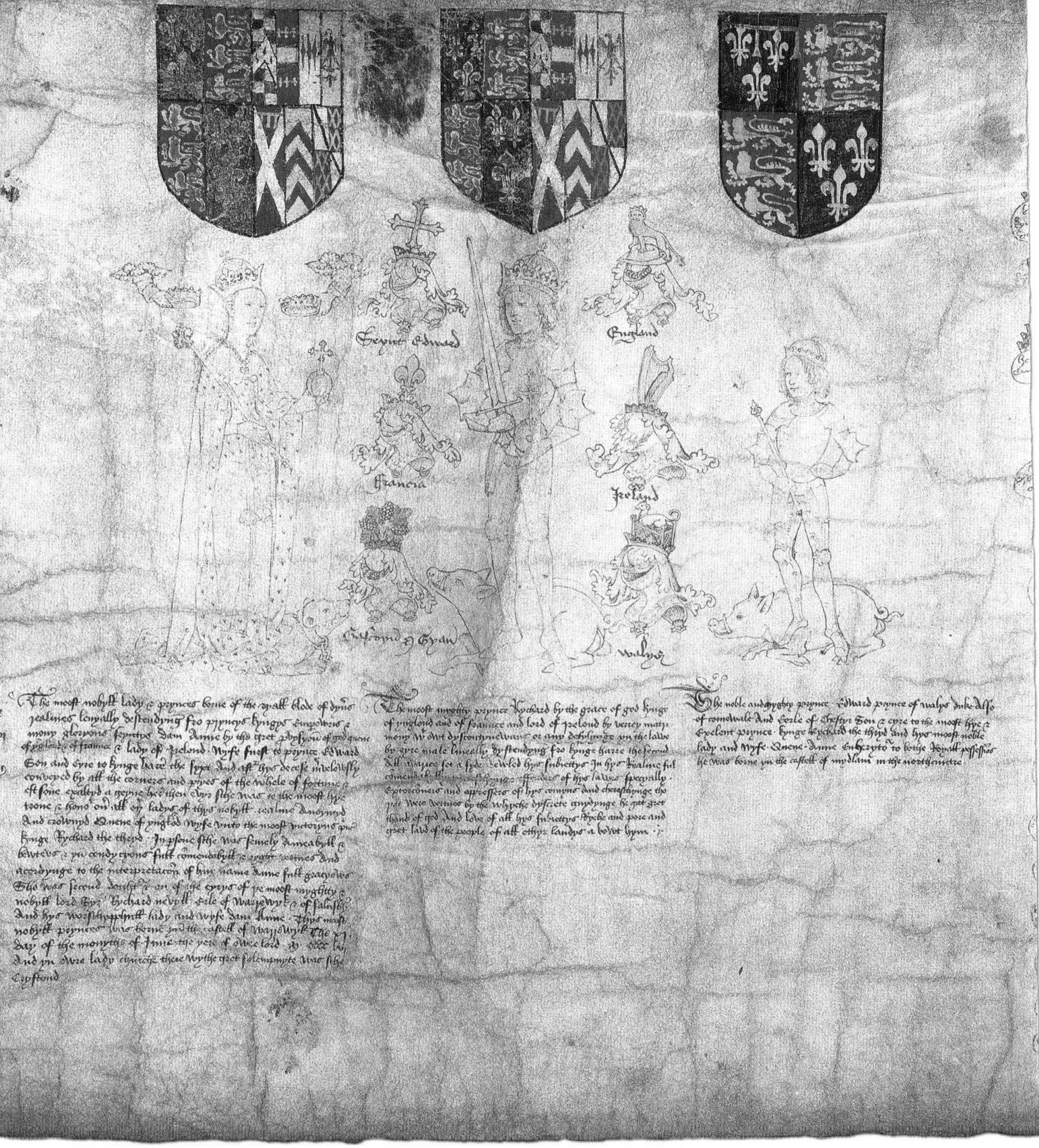


The most nobyll lady & pryncess borne of the ryall blode of dyvers realmes lenyally descendyng fro pryncys kyngys emperowrs & mony gloryous seyntys Dam Anne by the gret provysyon of god quene of ynglond & of fraunce & lady of Irelond wyfe furst to prynce Edward Son and eyre to kynge harre the syxt And aftr hys decese mervelously conveyed by all the corners and spyres of the whele of fortune & eftsone exaltyd a gayne hyer then evyr sche was to the most hye trone & hono{r} ou{r} all o{th}{er} ladys of thys nobyll realme Anoyntyd And crownyd Quene of ynglond wyfe vnto the most victoryus prynce kynge Rychard the thyrd In p{re}sence sche was semely Amyabyll & bewteus & yn condycyons full comendabyll & ryght vertuos And acordynge to the interpretacon of hur name Anne full gracyous Sche was second dowghtr & on of the eyrys of ye most myghty & nobyll lord Syr Rychard nevyll Erle of Warrewyk & of Salysbury And hys worschypfull lady and wyfe dam Anne. Thys most nobyll pryncess was borne in the castell of Warrwyk The xj day of the monyth of June the yere of owre lord M cccc lvj And yn owre lady churche there wythe gret solempnyte was sche crystend

The most myghty prynce Rychard by the grace of god kynge of ynglond and of fraunce and lord of Irelond by verrey matrimony w{i}t{h}owt dyscontynewans or any defylynge yn the lawe by eyre male lyneally dyscendyng fro kynge harre the second All avarice set a syde rewled hys subiettys yn hys realme ful comendabully punyschynge offenders of hys lawes specyally Extorcioners and oppressers of hys comyns and chereschynge tho that were vertues by the whyche dyscrete guydynge he gat gret thank of god and love of all hys subiettys ryche and pore and gret laud of the people of all othyr landys a bowt hym .

The noble and myghty prynce Edward prynce of walys duke also of cornewale And Erle of Chestyr Son & eyre to the most hye & Excelent prynce kynge Rychard the thyrd and hys most noble lady and wyfe Quene Anne Enherytor to bothe Ryall possessions he was borne yn the castell of mydlam in the northcuntre.

Laurence Olivier playing Richard III, with Ralph Richardson playing Buckingham, in the 1955 film of Shakespeare's play. A failure to separate the literary and historical Richard III by generations of historians has led to a merging of Shakespeare's characterization with the available historical evidence of Richard's actions and motives. The image of the scheming, deformed usurper is now firmly entrenched in popular culture.

literary exercise in exposing the consequences of leaving tyrants unchallenged. There was no reason to contribute anything that would enhance the reputation of the vanquished Richard III when the new Tudor dynasty faced enough problems.

The views of Vergil and More have persisted because they were the shared source material for many of the earliest printed histories of England, including Edward Hall's *Chronicle* (1548). Hall adapted and embellished Vergil's text, often with the sole purpose of defaming and undermining Richard's character. By creating a monstrous Richard III, Hall could justify Henry Tudor's usurpation in 1485 to a mid-Tudor audience worried about the strength of Edward VI's kingship.

When Shakespeare skilfully distilled Vergil, More and Hall's views of Richard, a deformed scheming monster was created. This image persists since it has been constantly reinterpreted on stage, film and television. The popularity of Shakespeare has meant that Laurence Olivier's portrayal of Richard in the 1955 film of the play was established as an archetype for medieval villains from the Sheriff of Nottingham to *The Black Adder*, and even Lord Farquaad in the children's film *Shrek*. As the *New York Times* put it in a review of 12 March 1956, Olivier created 'a weird poisonous portrait of a super-rogue whose dark designs are candidly acknowledged with lick-lip relish and sardonic wit'.

William Shakespeare is responsible for the popular modern image of Richard III. The success of his plays across the centuries has ensured that the dramatic Richard III has substituted the real historical figure. Richard as a haunted tyrant, punished by God for shedding innocents' blood, is an image found in many near-contemporary accounts of the reign. Shakespeare's sources, although developed during the Tudor period, absorbed real recollections and incorporated the testimonies of men and women alive before 1485: Tudor accounts of Richard III have a contemporary basis. The fundamental fact that Edward V and his brother disappeared while in his care has been enough to maintain the monstrous image of Richard III that has persisted since the end of the sixteenth century. Some historians therefore still see little difference between the literary and documented versions of Richard's life.

The Middleham boar badge. This hat badge was found in the drained moat of Middleham Castle. It has been suggested that Richard's use of the boar as an emblem may have arisen as a pun on the Latin name for his father's dukedom of York – *Eboracum*.

Since the 1920s, the Richard III Society has conducted a forceful campaign detailing the instances where Shakespeare's portrayal of Richard III departs from known facts. Most academics, too, have moved to a more moderate position. Very much work has now been completed on late fifteenth-century politics and culture, and Richard has been put back into the context of an aggressive society riven by feuding over land and influence. Historians now also understand more about the intentions of the Tudor literary sources previously relied upon as historical evidence. To some, however, Richard can still be dismissed as a dim and panicking usurper, and it is unlikely that the full legacy of Shakespeare's view will be fully overturned without the appearance of major new evidence.

## CONCLUSION: THE CONTINUING DEBATE

Despite strenuous attempts by the Richard III Society to reform his reputation, the image of Richard as a scheming, murdering hunchback persists, to varying degrees, in popular imagination and in the media today. Fundamentally, however, it must be accepted that Richard removed from power a child whom it was his sworn duty to protect. Whatever his provocations and the reasoning behind his course of action, this is the fact about Richard's reign that is hardest to dismiss.

Once Edward IV died, Richard acted with decisiveness and maintained the initiative, outmanoeuvring his opponents at every stage. In contrast to his father in 1459, Richard's own claim was announced at almost the same time as he deposed the King. In citing the conspiracies of his enemies as justification for his actions, Richard bemused contemporaries. There could be no independent verification of what he alleged, and Richard's swift decisions undermined opposition almost before it arose.

The appearance of the evidence supporting Richard's claim coincided with the unfolding of events and aroused suspicion, especially as the crucial facts of illegitimacy must have been suppressed within the Yorkist royal family. We have no evidence that Richard explored alternative means of preserving his status other than the most extreme option of deposing Edward V and eliminating his nephew's closest supporters.

That Richard chose not to follow these options makes it difficult to avoid the conclusion that, after the beginning of June 1483, he had every intention of becoming King. Whether he felt it was his right and duty, or that the opportunity to grasp the Crown was too great to ignore, the motivation behind Richard's accession remains the most enduring mystery of late medieval history.

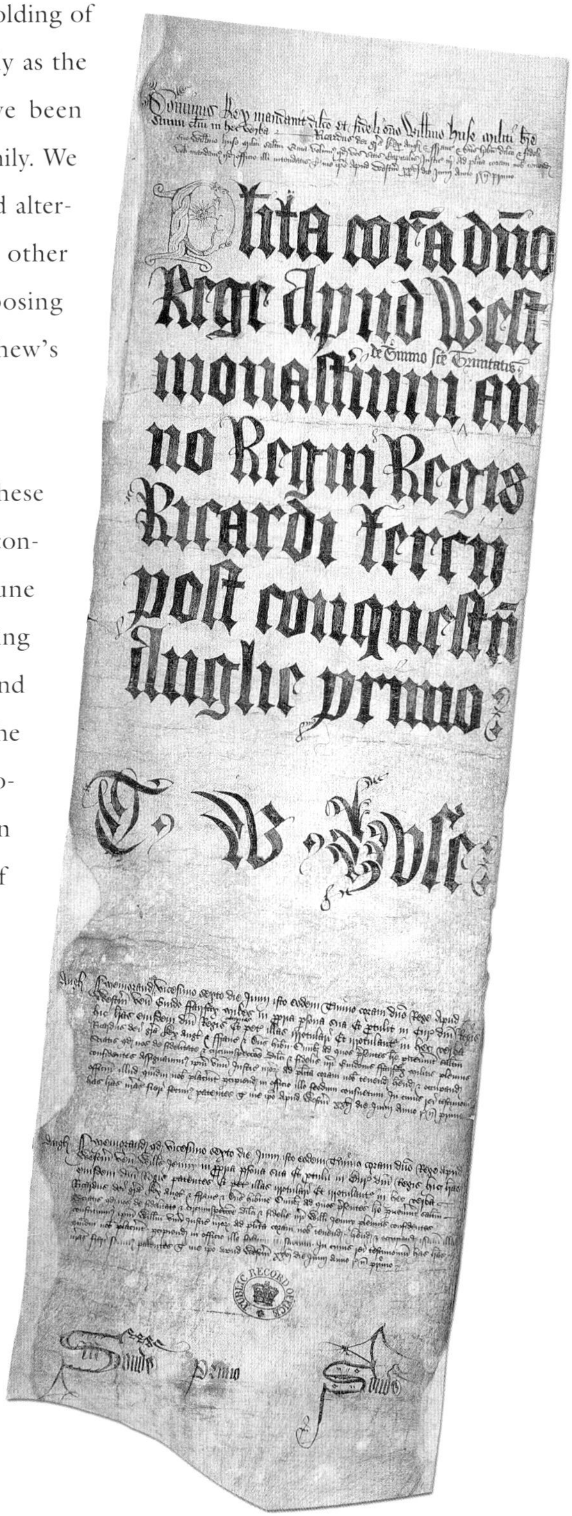

Court of King's Bench: *Coram Rege* Roll (Trinity Term, 1483). The King's (or Queen's) Bench was the senior common law court until 1875, and this document was a record of cases *coram rege* (before the king), i.e. those concerning criminal offences against the king's laws.

# Who's Who

**Queen Margaret of Anjou, 1430–82** Margaret married Henry VI in 1445, when aged about fifteen. She took advantage of Henry's mental breakdown to enter politics and sought the destruction of the claim of Richard, Duke of York. Margaret raised armies in 1460 and 1470 to challenge the Yorkists, and to promote her son Edward, Prince of Wales, but her forces were defeated in battle. In 1475, she returned to the care of her father, René, Duke of Anjou. He died in 1480; Margaret died destitute two years later.

**Margaret Beaufort, Countess of Richmond and Derby, 1443–1509** The mother of Henry Tudor; he was born when she was only thirteen years old and three months after the death of her husband, Edmund Tudor. Margaret was separated from her son when his wardship was granted to William Herbert, Earl of Pembroke in 1462. Margaret was married to Sir Humphrey Stafford by 1464, and Thomas, Lord Stanley by 1473. She perhaps saw her son during Henry VI's Readeption, but they were again separated when Henry fled into exile with his uncle Jasper (Earl of Pembroke) in 1471. Initially Margaret hoped to arrange his return as husband for one of Edward IV's daughters; but after Richard III's coronation, she began plotting with Elizabeth Woodville for Henry to become king. In conspiracy, she proved herself to be skilful and subtle, and upon Henry's accession she became his closest advisor and confidante. She received independent political power in the east midlands and was ruthless in enforcing loyalty to the new Tudor regime. Her religious life was exemplary and she rivalled Cecily Neville as a benefactor of religious houses. She also encouraged learning through patronage of printers and the establishment of colleges at Cambridge. Margaret outlived her son and oversaw the accession of Henry VIII. She was taken ill at his coronation festivities and died in June 1509.

**Henry Stafford, Duke of Buckingham, c. 1457–83** Buckingham was an ambitious and aggressive nobleman who shared many of Richard III's skills and aspirations. He did not enter politics until he reached his majority in 1473, but even as a teenager he was hungry for power and responsibility. His direct descent from Edward III's youngest son, Thomas of Woodstock, made Buckingham very conscious of his royal status, and he adopted Woodstock's arms and claimed part of the valuable Bohun inheritance from the Crown. His marriage to Elizabeth Woodville's sister Catherine gave the Duke a strong connection to the Yorkist royal family, even if it was shared by many other nobles during the 1470s. Nevertheless, he was left isolated by Edward IV, perhaps because of his youthful rashness and overt public display of his royal descent. But in an age where his contemporaries were assuming major responsibilities while still teenagers, his exclusion from power is telling. He was completely overlooked for membership of the Prince of Wales's Council of the Marches, when his regional landholding might have required him to head the Prince's household. The power of the Woodvilles in the Welsh Marches, and their dominance of Edward, Prince of Wales meant that Buckingham could achieve little until Woodville power was undermined. This prompted Buckingham's alliance with Richard, Duke of Gloucester in 1483. He proved himself to be able, eloquent and meticulous in helping Richard to the throne, and was rewarded with the most spectacular grant of lands, stewardships and power seen in medieval England. This gave him the authority usually enjoyed by the Prince of Wales and much more besides. Having achieved this, the only reasonable explanation for his rebellion against Richard in October 1483 was that he planned to seize the Crown, and used Henry Tudor as a distraction for his own intentions. With a massive landed base Buckingham probably hoped that the counties of the Welsh March would rise in support. He seriously miscalculated his appeal and a combination of poor coordination of uprisings across the south and appalling weather led to his capture and execution at Salisbury on 2 November 1483, aged only 26.

**George Plantagenet, Duke of Clarence, 1449–78** Brother of Edward IV and Richard III. He was murdered, allegedly in a barrel of wine, in the Tower in 1478. His death was the result of persistent disloyalty and treason, and the political faction fighting at the Yorkist court during the 1470s. Clarence had rebelled in 1469 and 1470, and allied himself with his brother's enemies Warwick and Queen Margaret. Edward's forgiveness was remarkable, and Clarence was able to submit and return to the King's favour. That he then continued to dabble in treason when under scrutiny for past disloyalty indicates his arrogant personality and, perhaps, his wish to be king. He had already proved himself capable of ruthlessness when, as a teenage duke, he pressed King Edward for grants of suitable estates in the 1460s. As husband of Isabel Neville, eldest co-heiress of Richard, Earl of Warwick, he also clashed bitterly with his brother Richard over the spoils of the Warwick inheritance in the early 1470s. Clarence inherited the earldom of Warwick through his wife, and in the west midlands showed that he could conduct himself as a benevolent and impartial regional good lord. Yet he could not come to terms with his status as a great noble and brother of the King. Despite great intelligence and articulate ability, his wish for greater prominence made him vulnerable to manipulation by the Woodville family, who are now credited with engineering his downfall. He was seen as an obstacle to their expanding influence, and Edward was persuaded to try and execute him in 1478. His son Edward, Earl of Warwick was the last great Plantagenet royal nobleman. For most of his life he was imprisoned by Henry VII, suspicious that he remained a focus for Yorkist plotting.

**Edward IV, 1442–83** Edward was the archetype of a medieval king. At the height of his abilities he was chivalrous and a great battlefield commander; very tall and attractive; honest and direct with his subjects; interested in good government for a stronger Crown, but not obsessive or avaricious. Following the disasters of Henry VI's reign, Edward restored the dignity and regality of the English monarchy by promoting himself and his family above the ranks of nobles from which he emerged. Through sound government he was able to achieve international acknowledgement of the legitimacy of Yorkist kingship. He sometimes lacked foresight and was easily swayed by the opinions of leading subjects who knew how his personal style of kingship worked. Edward's secret marriage and the subsequent influence of the Queen and her family upon him is the prime example of how his attention and focus could be distracted and manipulated. Edward allowed powerful figures such as Warwick, Richard of Gloucester, the Herberts and the Woodvilles, among others, to transform their existing regional power on the King's terms into semi-regal dominance. Their control threatened the political stability of the realm and was only held in check by Edward's ability to influence them himself. This personal style of ruling was remarkable and led to Edward memorizing an amazing array of detailed knowledge about his supporters, their families and landholdings. He was also actively involved in government processes, often checking grants and interviewing petitioners directly. Edward's greatest achievements came early in his reign as he established the Yorkist dynasty. As he became secure he also became comfortable in luxury. By his late thirties he was obese, despite being 6ft 4ins, and was more inclined to ignore problems or to act under the influence of others – the Woodville persecution of Clarence being but one example. His premature death did not cause the crisis that followed, but Edward must take responsibility for establishing the political structure that allowed his acknowledged heir to be deposed within three months.

**Edward V, 1470–?83** Edward IV's eldest son, who died uncrowned following his disappearance in June 1483. Edward was brought up during the 1470s under the influence of the Woodville family of his mother. His household at Ludlow was modelled on that of earlier Princes of Wales and gave him a suitable education. Edward showed himself to be intelligent, a good learner and possessed of the abilities required of a successful king. However, after his uncle Richard seized the Crown the young King was no longer seen in public. As a focus for conspiracy, it was believed at the time that Edward and his younger brother were killed before the end of 1483, and most probably with Richard's knowledge.

**Edward of Lancaster, Prince of Wales, 1453–71** The son of Henry VI and Queen Margaret, his birth changed the course of Henry VI's reign and prompted Richard, Duke of York into a more confrontational position. Edward gave the Lancastrian regime an heir and provided Queen Margaret with a political focus that her husband had failed to achieve. He accompanied his mother into exile in 1465 and was brought up in France. As a youth Edward strained to be given responsibility, but because of his importance as focus for all Lancastrians after Towton, Margaret protected him. By the age of seventeen, he was given command of the Lancastrian centre at the Battle of Tewkesbury in what should have been the climax of a coordinated campaign against Edward IV. Unfortunately Prince Edward was killed during the rout of the Queen's army. The death of Henry VI a few days later, placed Lancastrian hopes in the unlikely figure of Henry Tudor.

**Edward of Middleham, Prince of Wales, c. 1476–84** Richard III's son and heir who, from an early age, was groomed for major responsibility as Prince of Wales. Richard attempted to enforce the loyalty of the Lords and Commons to his heir in 1484, but Edward's early death removed this secure basis for Richard's kingship.

**William, Lord Hastings, c. 1438–83** Edward IV's leading follower, friend and political ally. He was a lifelong servant of the York family and a constant companion during Edward's numerous political crises and periods of exile. During Edward's reign, he was powerful in Leicestershire as steward of Tutbury Castle, but he also commanded Calais and the permanent army that garrisoned England's last continental possession. As Lord Chamberlain he controlled Edward's household and managed access to the King in person. This brought him into conflict with Queen Elizabeth's family, and especially her son Thomas Grey, Marquis of Dorset. He was accused by the Woodvilles of encouraging Edward's notorious womanising and other excesses, and was sufficiently vulnerable after Edward's death to seek allies such as Richard, Duke of Gloucester and Buckingham against Woodville influence. Hastings was passionate about preserving the Yorkist line and when it became clear that Edward V was to be deposed he may have planned to act against Richard, perhaps even in alliance with the Woodvilles, as Richard indeed alleged after 1483. Hastings's straightforward loyalty made him easy to predict and, as an alleged conspirator against Richard, he was summarily beheaded on 13 June 1483 as a prelude to Richard's seizure of the throne.

**Henry VI, 1421–71** Henry was the only child of Henry V, and became king as an infant in 1421. England was ruled successfully in his name until 1437 when Henry took control of government. The King's abilities did not match those required and he was inconsistent and influenced by his deeply religious outlook. This distraction allowed favourites such as William, Duke of Suffolk to take advantage of royal weaknesses. Lack of direction in policy allowed the gradual loss of almost all England's French possessions, as the French Crown asserted itself during the 1440s. Just after the birth of his only son, Edward, in 1453, Henry suffered a severe mental breakdown. This enabled Richard, Duke of York to assert his royal claims, and despite

Henry's partial recovery, faction and opposition emerged among the nobility, as peers scrambled to influence the weakened King. Henry became disinterested in anything but quiet piety, even ignoring the building projects at Eton and King's College, Cambridge that had obsessed him previously. He was a pawn in the events leading to the outbreak of civil war in 1455 and again in 1459. Queen Margaret became defender of the interests of Edward, Prince of Wales against the Yorkists, and Henry was a bystander in politics despite the loss of his Crown to Edward IV in March 1461. He was captured in 1465 but spared because the real Lancastrian threat lay with Prince Edward. Henry was placed back on the throne in September 1470, as a figurehead for the alliance of Warwick, Clarence and Queen Margaret, but following the Lancastrian disaster at Tewkesbury, Henry was murdered in the Tower on 21 May 1471, aged 49.

**Queen Anne Neville, 1456–85** Wife of Edward of Lancaster, Prince of Wales and, from 1472, of Richard, Duke of Gloucester. Her position as co-heiress of the Earl of Warwick delivered to Richard the northern Neville estates and the service of many of Warwick's retainers. Much of this benefited the development of Richard's northern power base, but it also came to restrict him, as he became too closely identified with his northern supporters once he was King. Following Anne's death early in 1485, loyalty to the Queen among former Neville retainers forced them to challenge Richard's possible re-marriage to his niece, Elizabeth of York.

**Cecily Neville, Duchess of York, 1415–95** As mother of the Yorkist kings, Cecily Neville was at the very top of the social scale in late medieval England. Cecily was the twenty-third child of Ralph, first Earl of Westmorland and Joan Beaufort, daughter of John of Gaunt. Her marriage to Richard Plantagenet, Duke of York was a suitable match between two families of great status. Cecily was a great beauty and indulged in the luxurious lifestyle that her marriage allowed. She also supported her husband's actions in claiming the Crown at the end of the 1450s, and moved beyond the role expected of contemporary noblewomen when she became directly involved in political events. After York died at the Battle of Wakefield in December 1460, and her son Edward became King, Cecily secured confirmation of her lands and rights, and as a wealthy widow she continued her pious patronage of religious houses. After 1461 she sought a suitable marriage for the King, but reacted angrily to Edward's secret marriage to Elizabeth Woodville in 1464, styling herself 'Queen by Right'. She may have been involved in promoting George, Duke of Clarence during Warwick's rebellion and the Readeption crisis of 1469–71. Cecily avoided court during Edward IV's second reign and concentrated on her private interests. She seems to have supported Richard III's seizure of the Crown, and may have known the truth of Richard's arguments over the illegitimacy of the Princes. Even after Richard's death she remained hostile to the Tudors, and some of her servants were active supporters of Perkin Warbeck at her death in 1495.

**John Howard, Duke of Norfolk, c. 1430–85** Rose to prominence through his descent from the Mowbray dukes of Norfolk. Through service to Thomas Mowbray, Duke of Norfolk, in France and Suffolk, and during the first phase of the Wars of the Roses, he earned his knighthood and service in Edward IV's household. Once connected to the Crown, Howard proved himself indispensable, working on overseas missions, in the royal Council and as a representative of the Crown in East Anglia. He was created Lord Howard in 1470 after standing by Edward IV during Warwick's first rebellion. The survival of his household account books give a very clear picture of a nobleman who paid great attention to his local interests connections and estates. This diligence was applied to his royal service, and following the extinction of the Mowbray line with the death of Anne, wife of Prince Richard, Duke of York, Howard became prominent in East Anglia, but the King kept the Mowbray lands. Like many others Howard saw the Woodville domination of Edward V as a major obstacle to what he felt was his rightful estate, and he backed Richard, Duke of Gloucester's accession. He was rewarded with the dukedom of Norfolk and remained loyal to Richard, dying for him at Bosworth. Norfolk's death allowed his direct opponent on 22 August, John de Vere, Earl of Oxford, to assume Howard's place as royal representative in East Anglia.

**Henry Percy, Earl of Northumberland, c. 1449–89** Percy recovered the northern influence of this great family following a long struggle with the Neville family. After the death of Richard, Earl of Warwick at Barnet in 1471, Percy was restored to the earldom of Northumberland, previously held by John Neville, Marquis of Montague. He came to an agreement with Richard, Duke of Gloucester in 1474 to protect his own affinity from Richard's dominant lordship. Northumberland then went on to serve Richard in the region, in the Scottish war of 1482 and backed his seizure of the throne in June 1483 with a large northern army. Richard's reliance upon the former Neville servants loyal to his wife meant that Northumberland could never achieve regional dominance while Richard's power was based in the north. Once king, Richard tried to extend his appeal, but even then, Northumberland was not given control of the Council of the North, and he may have resented the King's determination to delegate responsibility to trustworthy members of his family, such as his nephew John, Earl of Lincoln. Northumberland may have tried to exercise some form of revenge at Bosworth, where the northern retinues under his command were not committed to the fighting. This seems to have been remembered by the people of the north, and when Henry VII compelled Northumberland to confront tax protestors near Thirsk in 1489, he was abandoned by his servants and murdered by the mob.

**John de Vere, Earl of Oxford, c. 1443–1513** Oxford was the great survivor of the Wars of the Roses. He is often seen as implacably Lancastrian, and his father and brother had rebelled against Edward IV in 1462. However, Oxford's status as brother-in-law to Richard, Earl of Warwick both preserved his position during Edward's first reign, and also gave him the opportunity to rebel in 1469–70. He was a leading supporter of the Readeption of Henry VI and even after Tewkesbury he denied the legitimacy of the Yorkist King. He fled to France in 1471 but raided the English coast and captured St Michael's Mount in 1473. Oxford was captured and imprisoned at Hammes Castle in Calais, but in 1484 persuaded the constable Sir James Blount to allow his escape. He joined Henry Tudor's court in exile and commanded the Tudor forces at Bosworth. He was restored under Henry VII, and dominated East Anglia through his position at court and the eclipse of regional rivals the Howards and de la Poles. He proved himself an exceptional regional lord and attracted many of the gentry who had previously served his rivals. He accommodated the return to favour of Thomas Howard, Earl of Surrey after 1500 and continued to serve Henry VIII. His failure to produce a male heir ended the influence of the de Veres, as Howard and Charles Brandon were made dukes of Norfolk and Suffolk respectively in 1513.

**William Herbert, Earl of Pembroke, ex 1469** Herbert was Edward IV's representative in Wales and one of the most able and prominent Welshmen of the fifteenth century. Loyal service to Richard, Duke of York in the Welsh Marches during the 1450s, and successes against the Lancastrians in Wales during 1459–61, allowed him to make the smooth transition to service with Edward IV. He was given enormous authority by Edward and, as with many other nobles, married his son to one of the Queen's sisters. He remained loyal to Edward during Warwick's rebellion in 1469, and was captured at the Battle of Edgecote and immediately executed by Warwick.

**Anthony Woodville, Earl Rivers, c. 1442–83** A cultured and chivalric figure who stood out among his contemporaries for his lifestyle; he compiled the first book to be published by Caxton, and was an expert jouster. Rivers had little interest in practical administration and the application of royal policy, although his intellect meant that he did have the capacity to understand what was required. He found himself excluded from independent national office under his brother-in-law Edward IV for that reason. He was, however, given responsibility for educating Edward, Prince of Wales, and when surrounded by other royal officials of more practical skills his service was advantageous to the Crown. He did use his dominance over Prince Edward to advance himself and his relatives, and employed the deviousness and ruthlessness of fifteenth-century nobles to get what he wanted. Historians have often used the strong evidence of Rivers' cultural interests to explain his political detachment, which in turn made him susceptible to Richard's actions in April 1483. He was executed at Pontefract on the eve of Richard's accession in June 1483.

**Edmund Beaufort, Duke of Somerset, c. 1406–55** As grandson of John of Gaunt, Somerset was at the very centre of the Lancastrian regime. He inherited his title in 1444, but diligent service in France from the 1420s had already given him major lands and offices in England's French possessions. In 1446 he became English commander-in-chief in France, but his poor leadership allowed a sapping of English morale just as the French rallied and he oversaw the final English expulsion from France. Somerset did not possess great landed estates and depended on payments of fees and annuities from the Crown for most of his wealth. When Henry VI's government began to experience financial difficulties Somerset found his own resources pressurized. Somerset's conduct in France undermined his reputation and he clung to the court faction of William, Duke of Suffolk. This, and the failure of his military leadership, made him a focus for Richard, Duke of York's hostility. Henry VI did little to end royal support for Somerset, restoring him to favour after his bouts of insanity. This contributed towards the polarization of political factions and hastened York's move towards civil conflict to press his claims for reform of government. Somerset was killed at the first Battle of St Albans in 1455, but his death only heralded a further phase of revenge and recrimination among the nobility from 1459–61.

**Thomas, Lord Stanley, 1433–1504** Created Earl of Derby by Henry VII in 1485 for his family's support of the Tudor pursuit of the Crown. Thomas Stanley was a skilful and self-interested political manoeuverer. He had become Lord Stanley in 1459 yet changed political loyalties frequently to maintain his contacts with the shifting power behind Henry VI's Crown. His behaviour at the Battle of Blore Heath in September 1459 mirrored that at Bosworth twenty-six years later, when he stood apart from the main fighting, awaiting a suitable moment to intervene decisively. Unlike his partisan Yorkist brother Sir William Stanley, Lord Thomas seldom allowed political decisiveness to interrupt his steady accumulation of estates and influence in the north-west. As Warwick's brother-in-law, he supported the Readeption of Henry VI. His dispute with Richard, Duke of Gloucester over control of the Harrington heiresses and Hornby Castle conveniently prevented his attendance at either Barnet or Tewkesbury, but despite his military assistance to Warwick, he was quickly able to convince Edward IV of his intended good service to the restored Yorkist regime. One of Lord Stanley's achievements was to co-ordinate the various retinues of Stanley family members into a single coherent unit and they often used their neutrality to great effect, as witnessed during the 1483 rebellion against Richard. Lord Stanley's third marriage to Henry Tudor's mother Margaret Beaufort brought him to the brink of conspiracy and he was sufficiently suspected to be imprisoned after the fateful Council meeting on 13 June 1483. He may have managed military manoeuvres in Tudor's favour before Bosworth, but still did not engage in fighting – allowing his brother, who had already been declared a traitor by Richard, to take the risks on the battlefield. He retained the trust of Henry VII, but following his death in 1504, the Stanley family were targeted as dangerously overmighty subjects.

**Richard Neville, Earl of Salisbury and Warwick, 'the Kingmaker', 1428–71**
Warwick was the most powerful noble of the first period of Yorkist rule. Through marriage and inheritance he acquired vast estates in the west midlands and north and built his servants and interests to the point that he was able to influence who wore the Crown during the period 1460–71. Much like Richard, Duke of York (1411–60), he was very conscious of his own status and reacted badly to Edward IV's promotion of the Woodvilles and other newly ennobled families. Having secured the Crown for Edward in 1461, Warwick felt entitled to a position as leading councillor and came to expect that his advice would be heeded by his young King. When it was not, Warwick felt that he was being excluded. His disappointment at the King's marriage rankled, as did the rejection of his pro-French foreign policy. His gradual disillusionment emerged as rebellion in 1469 when he attempted to place Clarence on the throne. Warwick's desperation was shown by his alliance with his former enemy Margaret of Anjou, and the marriage of his daughter Anne to Henry VI's son Edward in 1470. Warwick was killed at the Battle of Barnet in April 1470, confirming that although he was a political kingmaker, he lacked the military abilities that really counted during the Wars of the Roses.

**Queen Elizabeth Woodville, c. 1440–92**
The attractive widow of the Lancastrian Sir John Grey, Elizabeth became the first English-born Queen for almost 300 years when she secretly married Edward IV in 1464. She used her position to secure land, income and advantageous marriages for her ten siblings. After Edward's death Woodville influence was challenged by the established peers; Elizabeth was sidelined, despite the marriage of her daughter Elizabeth to Henry VII in January 1486. She died in Bermondsey Abbey in 1492, aged about 52.

**Richard Plantagenet, Duke of York, 1411–60**
With two major lines of descent from Edward III, York had a strong claim to the Crown that he gradually pressed from the mid-1450s. He was one of the wealthiest peers of his age, and he and his wife Cecily Neville enjoyed extensive Welsh and Irish estates and an extravagant lifestyle. Under Henry VI, he was King's Lieutenant in France from 1436 and Ireland in 1446, but his personal abilities have been questioned – often relying on his status and the hard work of subordinates to achieve what was required. This mentality prompted numerous clashes with other nobles when he felt slighted or under-valued – most notably with the Beaufort family over command in France and payment for services. He did become Protector during Henry VI's periods of incapacity and gradually attracted enough support among his Neville relatives firstly to remove political rivals around the King, and then to challenge Henry VI's right to rule. In 1460 York claimed a superior hereditary right to the Crown, and although acknowledged as heir to Henry VI, his actions prompted Queen Margaret and her allies to renew civil war to defend Lancastrian interests. York's death at the Battle of Wakefield on 31 December 1460 allowed his eldest son Edward, Earl of March to assume the Yorkist claim, but as a unifier and not the destructive figure his father had been. He acceded as Edward IV on 4 March 1461.

**Richard Plantagenet, Duke of York, 1474–?83**
The youngest of the Princes in the Tower. Also known as Richard of Shrewsbury, he married the heiress Anne Mowbray in 1478. He was taken to sanctuary by his mother Elizabeth Woodville in May 1483, but was delivered to the care of his uncle, Richard Duke of Gloucester, soon after on 16 June. He was lodged in the Tower with his brother but was not seen following Richard's accession on 26 June.

# The Houses of York and Lancaster

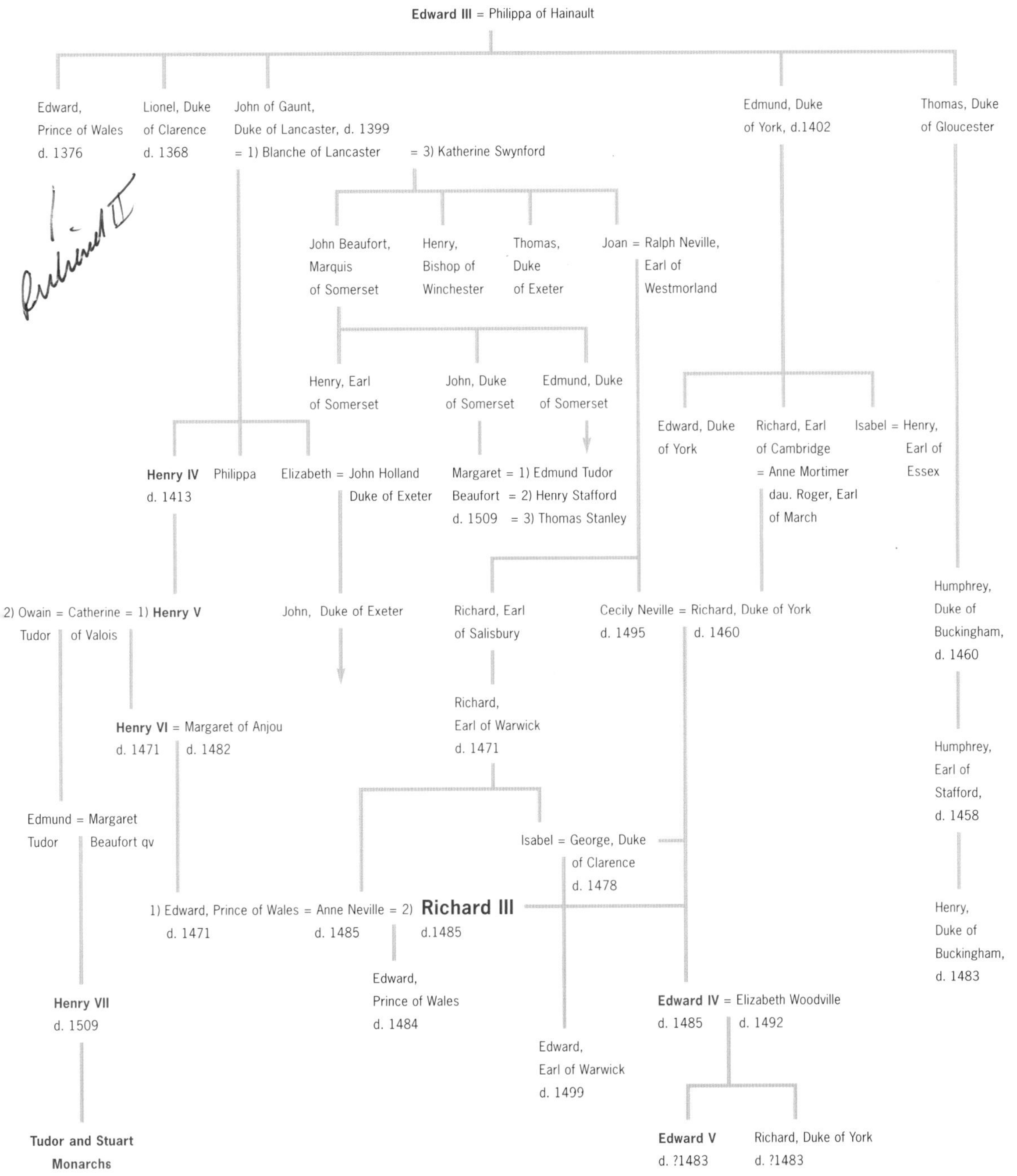
Edward III = Philippa of Hainault
Edward, Prince of Wales d. 1376
Lionel, Duke of Clarence d. 1368
John of Gaunt, Duke of Lancaster, d. 1399 = 1) Blanche of Lancaster = 3) Katherine Swynford
Edmund, Duke of York, d.1402
Thomas, Duke of Gloucester
John Beaufort, Marquis of Somerset
Henry, Bishop of Winchester
Thomas, Duke of Exeter
Joan = Ralph Neville, Earl of Westmorland
Henry, Earl of Somerset
John, Duke of Somerset
Edmund, Duke of Somerset
Edward, Duke of York
Richard, Earl of Cambridge = Anne Mortimer dau. Roger, Earl of March
Isabel = Henry, Earl of Essex
Henry IV d. 1413
Philippa
Elizabeth = John Holland Duke of Exeter
Margaret Beaufort d. 1509 = 1) Edmund Tudor = 2) Henry Stafford = 3) Thomas Stanley
2) Owain Tudor = Catherine of Valois = 1) Henry V
John, Duke of Exeter
Richard, Earl of Salisbury
Cecily Neville d. 1495 = Richard, Duke of York d. 1460
Humphrey, Duke of Buckingham, d. 1460
Henry VI d. 1471 = Margaret of Anjou d. 1482
Richard, Earl of Warwick d. 1471
Humphrey, Earl of Stafford, d. 1458
Edmund Tudor = Margaret Beaufort qv
Isabel = George, Duke of Clarence d. 1478
1) Edward, Prince of Wales d. 1471 = Anne Neville d. 1485 = 2) Richard III d.1485
Henry, Duke of Buckingham, d. 1483
Edward, Prince of Wales d. 1484
Henry VII d. 1509
Edward, Earl of Warwick d. 1499
Edward IV d. 1485 = Elizabeth Woodville d. 1492
Tudor and Stuart Monarchs
Edward V d. ?1483
Richard, Duke of York d. ?1483

# Chronology

1452 **2 October** Richard Plantagenet born at Fotheringhay, Northamptonshire.

1459 **12 October** Richard's father goes into exile after his defeat at the 'rout of Ludford'.

**November** Richard's father attainted in Parliament at Coventry.

1460 **March** Yorkist lords invade from Calais.

**10 July** Battle of Northampton: Henry VI captured by the Earl of Warwick.

**31 December** Battle of Wakefield: Richard's father, and brother Edmund, killed.

1461 **2 or 3 February** Battle of Mortimer's Cross; Edward, Earl of March claims throne and becomes Edward IV.

**17 February** Second Battle of St Albans: Warwick defeated.

**March** Richard and his brother George sent for protection to Philip, Duke of Burgundy.

**4 March** Edward IV proclaimed King in London.

**29 March** Yorkists crush Lancastrians at the Battle of Towton, near Tadcaster, Yorkshire.

**12 June** Richard and his brother George return to England.

**1 November** Richard made Duke of Gloucester.

1464 **May** Edward IV marries Elizabeth Woodville.

1465 **Autumn** Richard resident in the household of the Earl of Warwick.

1469 **January** Richard returns to court.

**June** Warwick's rebellion starts.

**29 July** Battle of Edgecote, near Banbury, Oxfordshire.

**17 October** Richard made Constable of England.

| | | |
|---|---|
| **1470** | **12 March** Warwick rebels again. Battle of Losecote Field; Warwick and Clarence flee and ally themselves with Henry VI. |
| **1470** | **26 August** Richard appointed warden of the West March towards Scotland. |
| | **September** Warwick invades with French help. Collapse of Edward IV's authority. |
| | **2 October** Richard accompanies Edward IV into exile. Restoration of King Henry VI. |
| **1471** | **March** Edward IV and Richard land in East Yorkshire. |
| | **14 April** Battle of Barnet: Warwick killed in defeat. |
| | **4 May** Battle of Tewkesbury: Edward IV defeats an invading Lancastrian army, Henry VI's son, Edward, Prince of Wales killed. |
| | **21 May** Henry VI murdered in the Tower of London. |
| **1472** | **Spring** Richard marries Warwick's daughter Anne Neville. Develops his northern dominance as political heir of Warwick. |
| **1475** | **29 August** Meeting at Picquingy between Edward IV and Louis XI ends England's invasion of France. |
| **1478** | **18 February** George, Duke of Clarence murdered in the Tower after his conviction for treason. |
| **1482** | **24 August** Berwick recovered during Richard's invasion of Scotland. |
| **1483** | **9 April** Death of Edward IV, succession of Edward V. |
| | **30 April** Richard and Buckingham arrest Rivers, Grey and Vaughan at Stony Stratford and secure custody of Edward V. |
| | **4 May** George Neville, Duke of Bedford dies, Richard loses hereditary hold on northern Neville lands. |
| | **7 May** A meeting of executors refuses to prove Edward IV's will. |
| | **10 June** Richard orders troops from the north. |

| | |
|---|---|
| 1483 | **13 June** Execution of Lord Hastings. Arrest of Stanley, Morton and Archbishop Rotherham. |
| | **16 June** Richard removes Richard, Duke of York from sanctuary at Westminster Abbey. |
| 1483 | **22 June** Richard's right to be King proclaimed in a sermon by Ralph Shaw. |
| | **26 June** Richard becomes King. |
| | **29 August** Richard arrives in York on progress. His accession is celebrated. |
| | **10 October** Rebellion across southern England aims to restore Edward V. |
| | **2 November** Execution of Buckingham at Salisbury. |
| 1484 | **23 January** Richard's only Parliament meets at Westminster. |
| | **April** Death of Edward of Middleham, Prince of Wales. |
| | **7 December** Proclamation against Henry Tudor. |
| 1485 | **9 June** Richard arrives at Nottingham awaiting Tudor's landing. |
| | **7 August** Tudor lands at Milford Haven in west Wales. |
| | **18 August** Richard's army mustered at Leicester. |
| | **22 August** Battle of Bosworth: Richard killed and Henry VII succeeds. |
| 1486 | **Easter** Rebellion at York, Henry VII almost captured. |
| 1487 | **16 June** Battle of Stoke: Henry VII defeats Richard's nephew, John, Earl of Lincoln. |
| 1491 | **November** Appearance of Perkin Warbeck in Ireland. Claims to be the youngest of the Princes in the Tower, Richard, Duke of York. |
| 1506 | **24 April** Richard III's nephew Edmund, Earl of Suffolk imprisoned in the Tower. Henry VII finally free from Yorkist conspiracy. |

# Further Reading


M. J. Bennett, ***The Battle of Bosworth*** (Alan Sutton, 1985). A very clear account of the battle.

J. Gillingham (ed.), ***Richard III: A Medieval Kingship*** (Collins & Brown, 1993). Quality essays from leading historians. Introduces Richard's life and reign to general readers.

M. A. Hicks, ***Richard III*** (Tempus, 2000). A new general biography that incorporates a great deal of original research.

R. Horrox, ***Richard III: A Study of Service*** (Cambridge University Press, 1988). A clear and expert analysis of how Richard ruled and why he failed to keep the Crown. The best book yet on Richard's reign.

R. Horrox (ed.), ***Richard III and the North*** (University of Hull, 1986). A collection of essays exploring Richard's relationship with northern society.

R. Horrox and P. W. Hammond (eds), ***British Library Harleian Manuscript 433*** 4 vols (Richard III Society/Alan Sutton, 1979–83). Fascinating original evidence of Richard's government at work. The major resource for his reign.

J. Hughes, ***The Religious Life of Richard III*** (Sutton, 1997). Assesses the impact of religion and piety upon Richard's career and personality.

M. K. Jones, ***Bosworth 1485: Psychology of a Battle*** (Tempus, 2002). The most challenging book to appear on Richard recently. Analyses motivations, investigates Yorkist illegitimacy and re-sites the battle.

Dominic Mancini, ***The Usurpation of Richard III*** tr. and ed. C. A. J. Armstrong (Oxford University Press, 1969, reprinted Sutton, 1986). A crucial eyewitness account of events in London during the early summer of 1483.

A. J. Pollard, ***North-Eastern England During the Wars of the Roses*** (Oxford University Press, 1990). A comprehensive study of the region and effects of civil war from 1450 to 1509.

A. J. Pollard, ***Richard III and the Princes in the Tower*** (Alan Sutton, 1991). A vigorous study of the central mystery of Richard's reign. Wonderfully illustrated and detailed.

C. D. Ross, ***Richard III*** (Methuen, 1981). The standard modern biography. Still the best scholarly account of the King.

A. F. Sutton and P. W. Hammond (eds), ***Richard III: Loyalty, Lordship and Law, 2nd edn*** (Sutton, 2000). A revised version of a collection from leading scholars first produced in 1985. Some essential essays included here.

# Picture Credits

**Illustrations**

Cover: National Portrait Gallery London; pp. i and x © Society of Antiquaries of London; p. ii by permission of The British Library (Additional MS 48976, nos. 62, 63, 64); p. 2 Bibliothèque Nationale, Paris, France/Bridgeman Art Library; p. 4 Collections/Roy Stedall-Humphreyes; p. 5 Musée Thomas Dobree-Musée Archéologique, Nantes, France/Bridgeman Art Library (Ms.18 f. 109v); p. 6 British Library, London, UK/Bridgeman Art Library; p. 7 Collections/Roy Stedall-Humphreyes; p. 10 British Library, London, UK/Bridgeman Art Library; p. 15 Bibliothèque Centrale, Ghent, Belgium/Bridgeman Art Library; p. 16 Private Collection/Bridgeman Art Library; p. 17 Collections/Pete Foot; p. 18 © Society of Antiquaries of London; p. 20 © Sonia Halliday Photographs; p. 21 Collections/Roy Stedall-Humphreyes; p. 26 Lambeth Palace Library, London, UK/Bridgeman Art Library; p. 28 by permission of the Duke of Buccleuch (from the Writhes Garter Book); p. 32 British Library, London, UK/Bridgeman Art Library; p. 33 © Sonia Halliday Photographs (photo: Bryan Knox); p. 36 © Geoffrey Wheeler; p. 45 Collections/Brian Shuel; p. 48 Victoria & Albert Museum, London, UK/Bridgeman Art Library; p. 52 Collections/Philip Craven; p. 53 Private Collection/Bridgeman Art Library; p. 57 by permission of the Master and Fellows of St John's College, Cambridge; p. 62 by permission of The British Library (MS Harley 4632, f. 242); p. 65 © Geoffrey Wheeler; p. 68 © Geoffrey Wheeler; p. 69 Wallace Collection, London, UK/Bridgeman Art Library p. 74 © Geoffrey Wheeler; p. 84 Bibliothèque Municipale, Arras, France/Bridgeman Art Library; p. 85 © Geoffrey Wheeler; pp. 86 and 96 © Society of Antiquaries of London; p. 89 © Geoffrey Wheeler; p. 92 Private Collection/Bridgeman Art Library; p. 97 © Society of Antiquaries of London; p. 100 The Kobal Collection/Olivier Productions/London Films/Big Ben Films; p. 101 York Museums Trust (Yorkshire Museum)

All other images are from The National Archives: Cover and pp. v and 103 KB 27/888/2; cover (background) C 81/1392/6; p. iii DL 10/392; p. 24 E 36/276; pp. 27 and 72–3 E 42/540; pp. 30–1 MPF 1/148; pp. 40–1 MR 1/16; p. 59 C 81/1531; p. 78 KB 27/956

Picture research by Deborah Pownall.

**Original documents**

Documents 2, 11, 16, and 18 are reproduced by permission of the British Library. All other documents are held in The National Archives.

# Index

Page references to illustrations are in *italics*; page references to documents are in **bold**.